Helion & Company Limited
Unit 8 Amherst Business Centre
Budbrooke Road
Warwick
CV34 5WE
England
Tel. 01926 499 619
Email: info@helion.co.uk
Website: www.helion.co.uk
Twitter: @helionbooks
Visit our blog http://blog.helion.co.uk/

Published by Helion & Company 2021
Designed and typeset by Farr out Publications, Wokingham, Berkshire
Cover designed by Paul Hewitt, Battlefield Design (www.battlefield-design.co.uk)

ISBN 978-1-914377-13-6

British Library Cataloguing-in-Publication Data
A catalogue record for this book is available from the British Library

We always welcome receiving book proposals from prospective authors.

CONTENTS

ABBREVIATIONS

ASP	Assistant Superintendent of Police
BDF	Barbados Defence Force
BGVF	British Guyana Volunteer Force
BPF	Barbados Police Force
CARICOM	Caribbean Community
CDS	Chief of Defence Staff
CLO	Central Liaison Office
CO	Commanding Officer
CoE	Commission of Enquiry
GDF	Guyana Defence Force
GEB	Guard and Emergency Branch
GNS	Guyana National Service
GPF	Guyana Police Force
GPM	Guyana Peoples Militia
GPMG	General Purpose Machine Gun
ISIS	Islamic State of Iraq and Syria
JAM	Jamaat – Jamaat-al-Muslimeen
JCF	Jamaica Constabulary Force
JDF	Jamaica Defence Force
JLP	Jamaica Labour Party
NHSL	National Helicopter Services Limited
PC	Police Constable
PNM	People's National Movement
PNP	People's National Party
PPP	People's Progressive Party
RBDF	Royal Bahamas Defence Force
RBPF	Royal Bahamas Police Force
RSS	Region Security System
SLR	Self Loading Rifle
SNU	Special Naval Unit
SRP	Special Reserve Police
SSU	Special Service Unit
TTCG	Trinidad and Tobago Coast Guard
TTDF	Trinidad and Tobago Defence Force
TTPS	Trinidad and Tobago Police Service
TTR	Trinidad and Tobago Regiment
UNC	United National Congress
WIR	West India Regiment

1 INTRODUCTION – THE ENGLISH-SPEAKING CARIBBEAN

The Caribbean region is an amalgam of islands and mainland states. With an intriguing mix of former and current colonies, English, Spanish, French and Dutch colonial pasts and an ethnic mix that includes almost every ethnicity and religion from every part of the globe. However, it should be stated that most of the countries in question have populations that are overwhelmingly of African descent. However, Trinidad and Tobago and Guyana have very large Indian populations – the largest single ethnic group in each case – and the racial mix in the latter two countries has presented its own political and social challenges as will be alluded to in the respective chapters.

The English-speaking Caribbean in particular has been more or less a bastion of democracy with only two countries – Grenada (for a four year period) and Guyana (with a rather more unfortunate period of 28 years of rigged elections) – having subverted their democratic traditions. The others remain committed to Westminster style democratic governance and have independent judiciaries and armed forces which have not sought to usurp power.

This introductory chapter will provide a brief background into the region's socio-economic multi-lateral structure, CARICOM in particular, and examine, briefly, the foreign policy and influences that have shaped the security policies of the region. The region's security challenges shall be outlined while the sources of arms supply are discussed with a view to contextualising the varied systems in use, while at the same time highlighting the growing Chinese influence as well as the near domination of the Dutch company, Damen Shipyards Group, as a supplier of naval vessels in the region.

CARICOM

The Caribbean Community is one of the landmark achievements of the Caribbean region and has been the brainchild of its English-speaking members though it now encompasses both Haiti and Suriname – former French and Dutch colonies respectively. Modelled loosely on the European Economic Community, CARICOM has also suffered from some of the post-Brexit anxieties, further exacerbated by its failure to evolve into an effective commercial or political entity.

It is hard to overstate the importance of the European model to the CARICOM project. There are enormous disparities in terms of population and wealth among its 15 member states (see Table 1).

Formed on 1 August 1973, with the purpose of fostering economic cooperation and integration and to coordinate foreign policy,[1] CARICOM was largely inspired from the European Economic Community (EEC) of the 1970s and subsequently by its transformation into the EU.[2] It is interesting to note that at no point of time was there any referendum in any Caribbean nation to either endorse or reject any aspect of this attempt at regional integration.

Since 2013, CARICOM and the Dominican Republic, collectively called Cariforum, have been the beneficiaries of an Economic Partnership Agreement (EPA) with the EU. This has given the region duty- and quota-free access to EU markets for all products, plus significant aid to boost trade, with gradual reciprocity being shown for EU exports to the region.[3]

The fate of the West Indies Federation still resonates among some of the countries in the region. Lasting from 1958 to 1962, the Federation was an attempt to create a unified Caribbean state as Britain granted independence to ten islands of the English-speaking Caribbean region. As independence drew near, Jamaica, which did not view its national interest as best served by establishing a unified Caribbean nation, withdrew from the Federation, prompting Trinidad to do the same. The expression coined by the then Trinidadian Prime Minister Eric Williams – 'one from ten leaves

Table 1: CARICOM Member States

State	Joined	Population	km²	GNI in US$ billion	GNI per capita in US$
Antigua and Barbuda	4 July 1974	91,818	442	1.2	12,910
Bahamas	4 July 1983	383,054	13,939	8.4	22,312
Barbados	1 August 1973 (Founder)	283,380	431	4.2	15,172
Belize	1 May 1974	351,706	22,966	1.6	4,660
Dominica	1 May 1974	72,341	750	0.493	6,760
Grenada	1 May 1974	106,349	345	0.806	7,460
Guyana	1 August 1973 (Founder)	763,893	216,960	3.1	3,750
Haiti	2 July 2002	10,572,029	27,560	8.766	820
Jamaica	1 August 1973 (Founder)	2,720,554	10,991	13.7	5,220
Montserrat	1 May 1974	4,900	103	0.058	11,836
Saint Kitts and Nevis	26 July 1974	54,944	269	0.724	13,460
Saint Lucia	1 May 1974	183,645	616	1.3	7,090
Saint Vincent and the Grenadines	1 May 1974	109,360	389	0.722	6,580
Suriname	4 July 1995	538,248	163,820	5.297	9,583
Trinidad and Tobago	1 August 1973 (Founder)	1,354,438	5,128	21.2	15,760

Source: International Monetary Fund, World Bank, CARICOM

nought', is still remembered whenever the concept of a unified Caribbean is discussed.

International Relations and Alliances

The countries of the English-speaking Caribbean are notionally non-aligned but are signatories to the Rio Treaty and the US Caribbean Basin Initiative provides a great deal of security assistance to CARICOM nations. The region was traditionally ideologically aligned to the West but now a Chinese push for influence in the region has created a new and interesting dynamic which is posing a challenge to the United States.

The United Kingdom and the United States remain important allies and very important trading partners, along with the countries of the European Union. However, these countries have diminishing political influence owing to their preoccupation with matters outside of the region. The CARICOM region has good relations with India, but these are symbolic and limited to cultural and some economic interaction.

China, however, is now easily the most active major power in seeking to cultivate influence in the region. In June 2013, during the visit of Chinese President Xi Jinping to Trinidad and Tobago, the then Prime Minister of the Caribbean nation, Kamla Persad-Bissessar, in a fawning speech, had lauded President Xi's vision saying, 'We see in your China Dream a splendid opportunity for China to become a model for the world.'[4] Like royalty holding court, President Xi thereafter hosted the leaders of Antigua and Barbuda, Barbados, the Bahamas, Dominica, Grenada, Guyana, Suriname and Jamaica in Port of Spain – capital of Trinidad and Tobago – where he announced soft loans and investments worth US$ 3 billion as well as grants of up to US$ 8 million for the region.[5] President Xi's visit was an effective and a graphic demonstration of China's growing influence and outreach in the English-speaking Caribbean region, coming at a time when the United States (US) had been somewhat less forthcoming with financial grants for the region.

Compared to the US, which has been wary of providing large-scale bilateral financial support due to endemic corruption in the Caribbean nations, the Chinese appear less concerned about such issues, thus further enhancing their prospects among the governing elites of the region where lack of transparency enables potentially shadowy deals between them to flourish.[6]

Regional Security Concerns

The English-speaking Caribbean is not a heavily militarised region. The main threats to the security and stability of the region come from internal threats from organised crime or insurgent groups that may be motivated by religious ideology.

Internal Security Challenges

The primary security challenge in the region is that of narcotics trafficking and the criminal gangs associated with such activity. In both Trinidad and Tobago and Jamaica, these gangs have emerged as major security challenges. For example, one of the more recent, and certainly most notorious, incidents being the 2010 operations against the 'Shower Posse' drug gang in an attempt to arrest its leader Christopher 'Dudus' Coke. These operations saw Jamaican police and defence forces engaged in urban combat with some 500 armed gang members in which four security personnel and 73 civilians lost their lives in a heavy exchange of fire in the ghettos of Kingston.

In Trinidad and Tobago, there is an additional challenge of radical Islamic activity. This was graphically brought to the fore in 1990 when one such group staged a coup attempt that held the then government hostage for six days. More recently, a large number of Trinidadian nationals left to fight in Syria and Iraq, often taking their wives and children with them, as part of the malevolent terrorist group Islamic State of Iraq and Syria (ISIS)/Daesh.

It is an unfortunate fact that nearly all major political parties in the Caribbean have flirted with criminal gangs to provide election muscle at different times, with the reward being the grant of lucrative government contracts to the leadership of those groups. These contracts, aimed at building infrastructure and at alleviating unemployment have used the money from these contracts to enrich themselves and recruit additional personnel, and through their ability to dispense patronage, have become powerful forces within their communities, with the wealth skimmed from the said contracts providing lavish lifestyles and the ability to wield influence that comes from a combination of muscle and money.

The gangs, by their presence and the image they cultivate, have been able to serve as a potential source of personnel for ISIS in Trinidad as extremist leaders of these criminal gangs are able to direct aspiring, impressionable and motivated recruits towards extremist ideology. In Jamaica, the gangs create a mystique of their own with a 'Robin Hood' story that makes them folk heroes These gangs, embedded in the urban neighbourhoods of the country and targeting vulnerable youth are in a position to exert maximum influence over their communities and, as has been noted above, they have no problem recruiting large numbers of 'soldiers' to carry out their wishes.

It would appear that despite billions of dollars in social programmes and welfare systems being spent, these programmes have failed to stop the creation of a sizeable pool of disaffected youth, ready to be swayed by the rhetoric and ideology of these extremist/criminal gangs. These gangs are reasonably well-armed, with the Jamaican gangs being able to contest the control of the streets against the Jamaican police.

Trinidad and Tobago and Jamaica are the worst afflicted by this criminal gang violence. Guyana, on the other hand, has problems of a different nature, partly due to its own criminal gang problem but exacerbated by the availability of weapons from old government stocks. This has led to violent attacks in both urban and rural Guyana. As such, the armed forces of these three countries have a pronounced internal security bias. In contrast, the rest of the English-speaking Caribbean does not face as severe a challenge from armed criminal gangs, thus allowing a less intense military involvement in internal security.

Small Militaries

Other than Guyana which faces a potentially existential threat from the much larger Venezuelan military, and possibly Trinidad and Tobago which has issues over maritime border transgressions and illegal migration from Venezuela, no country in the English-speaking Caribbean faces an external threat. Unsurprisingly, given the small size of the countries as well as their limited resources, only a few – Bahamas, Barbados, Guyana, Jamaica and Trinidad and Tobago – maintain dedicated military forces of any size and of these, only the last three operate land forces of any meaningful capability, and air assets of some limited but useful operational capability. The other CARICOM states operate police forces, usually unarmed but having paramilitary Special Service Units (SSUs) which have light infantry weapons and equipment and some quasi-military training.

An exception is Antigua & Barbuda which operates a tiny military of 245 personnel in the form of the Antigua & Barbuda Defence Force which has a small 'battalion' of company-plus size and a coast guard with three vessels. Grenada once possessed a substantial military but following Operation Urgent Fury in 1983, the country no longer has a separate military, with the police – the Royal Grenada Police Force (RGPF) – taking over the limited military functions through its Special Service Unit which is well-equipped with M16/M4 rifles and M60 machine guns as well as basic, non-lethal, riot control equipment. Dominica created a small defence force in 1975 but this was at loggerheads with successive elected governments and was disbanded in 1981 after rumours of coup attempts, smuggling of weapons and narcotics, as well as a seeming disrespect for the elected government which proved to be insurmountable.

Regional Security Structures

CARICOM does not operate any joint military forces and the defence forces of the individual countries are resolutely separate, to the extent of having minimal equipment compatibility. However, there is one joint security entity that has stood the test of time and has performed well whenever called upon. This is the Regional Security System (RSS) which details its history and mission as follows:

> The Regional Security System (RSS) was created out of a need for a collective response to security threats, which were impacting on the stability of the region in the early 1970s and 1980s. In October 1982, four members of the Organisation of the Eastern Caribbean States, namely, Antigua & Barbuda, Dominica, St. Lucia and St. Vincent and the Grenadines, signed a Memorandum of Understanding (MOU) with Barbados to provide for 'mutual assistance on request'. St. Kitts and Nevis joined after gaining independence in September 1983 and Grenada in January 1985. The MOU was updated in 1992 and the RSS acquired juridical status in March 1996 by way of the Treaty which was signed in St. Georges, Grenada.[7]

The RSS does not include either Jamaica, Guyana or Trinidad and Tobago though all three countries have collaborated with the RSS on occasion. Jamaica, for example, contributed troops to Urgent Fury, at least partly coordinated through the RSS, and Trinidad and Tobago benefitted enormously when CARICOM troops, coordinated through the RSS, arrived to assist with law and order duties in the aftermath of the 1990 coup. Another major function of the RSS is to provide coordination in respect of disaster relief operations, this being most recently done in Dominica following the devastation of Hurricane Maria in 2017.

However, although the RSS has at its disposal two C-26 aircraft for maritime surveillance, of which one is usually serviceable, the organisation has no troops attached to it and is dependent on the contributions from member nations as well as assistance from Trinidad and Jamaica, both of whom have substantial military forces and which have the ability to deploy military assets some distance from their national borders.

The RSS Air Wing was established in 1999, with two C-26 aircraft donated by the United States, as part of a wider package which saw two similar aircraft delivered to Trinidad. The first aircraft, which was not fitted with a sensor package, was delivered to Barbados in January 1999. It was used for training and logistics missions. The second aircraft, with a full sensor package was delivered in 2001. The first aircraft was subsequently upgraded with a similar surveillance package.[8]

Grenada 1983 – The First Test[9]

The US intervention in Grenada in 1983 warrants a book all on its own. In summary, in October 1983, a military coup ousted the left-leaning, Cuban inspired, Prime Minister Maurice Bishop from power, executed him and a number of his cabinet ministers and perhaps up to eight Grenadian civilians who tried to rescue Bishop, with at least 100 more civilians being wounded. The Revolutionary Military Council (RMC) formed on 19 October 1983, ostensibly under the leadership of General Hudson Austin, but in reality under the de facto control of a faction of Soviet-supported members of Bishop's New JEWEL Movement led by Bernard Coard, was met with regional disapproval and as the RMC tightened its grip on power, foreign intervention was sought and, with the support of the Organisation of Eastern Caribbean States (OECS), the United States intervened with fighting lasting from 25 October to 29 October 1983, leading to the overthrow of the RMC and the restoration of democracy to the island.

The RSS played an important role in coordinating the OECS military response and seven CARICOM countries sent security personnel to assist. Jamaica sent some 150 troops, Barbados 50 and Antigua and Barbuda sent a single infantry squad. Other members, Dominica, St Lucia, St Vincent and the Grenadines, and St Kitts and Nevis, plus Barbados, sent police or members of their police SSUs to form a Caribbean Peacekeeping Force (CPKF) of some 350 personnel.

The roles played by the Jamaica and Barbados defence forces will be examined in their respective chapters but the 1983 Grenada intervention showed that the RSS was capable of performing a significant coordination role for operations within the region.

Assisting Trinidad in 1990

On 27 July 1990, a radical Islamic group, the Jamaat-al-Muslimeen attempted a violent overthrow of the elected government of Trinidad and Tobago. While details of the coup and the response by local forces will be detailed in the chapter on Trinidad, the CARICOM and the RSS, through its Central Liaison Office (CLO), were prepared to assist. By 11:30 p.m. on 27 July 1990, all CARICOM defence forces and police Special Service Units (SSUs) were placed on alert for possible deployment to Trinidad.[10]

The Jamaica Defence Force prepared a full rifle company of five officers and 123 men for deployment while the Barbados Defence Force prepared three platoons with three more requested from the Antigua and Barbuda Defence Force (A&BDF). The police SSUs from all participating islands were requested to provide 20 men each with Grenada being asked for 30. However, the A&BDF and the police forces of Dominica and St Kitts were unable to meet these requests, with the A&BDF eventually despatching only a single rifle section of 12 men to Trinidad.[11]

For 24 hours the RSS had no clue as to the ground situation in Trinidad and plans were made to muster forces in Grenada to be transported by three RSS vessels – the *Tyrell Bay*, the *Captain Mulzac* and the *George Mackintosh* – to Trinidad. These vessels being of modest size, would require several trips to transport even the limited forces being mustered.[12]

The CARICOM forces had significant shortfalls in equipment and communications gear with radios and even ammunition being in short supply. The United States was asked to assist to make good the shortfalls.[13] This was less pronounced in the case of Jamaica and Barbados but the police SSUs were desperately short of equipment.

Communications with the Trinidad and Tobago Defence Force (TTDF) were established at 10:45 a.m. on 28 July via telephone with Colonel Ralph Brown's office after which a High Frequency link was established by the Trinidad and Tobago Coast Guard (TTCG) to the CLO on 8.645 MHz with Commander Richard Kelshall delivering a thorough briefing at 11:00 a.m.[14] However, in the event, the TTDF was able to contain the situation with its own resources and the CARICOM troops, which arrived later, were assigned to augment the battered Trinidad and Tobago Police Service and to assist in the guarding of vital infrastructure points. Nonetheless, the willingness of CARICOM to assist remains noteworthy, despite the limited capabilities and resources available to the individual armed forces. It should be noted that the acute shortage of air transport remains a problem.

Hurricane Maria – The RSS and CARICOM's Finest Hour[15]

Following the devastation of Dominica by Hurricane Maria, and in a display of regional solidarity coordinated by the Caribbean Disaster Emergency Management Agency (CDEMA), Dominica's fellow CARICOM members rallied to her aid. CDEMA, an inter-regional network of the disaster management agencies of the CARICOM member states, facilitated a response by the defence forces of Trinidad and Tobago, Jamaica and Barbados which spearheaded the relief effort, later assisted by an invaluable contribution from the Bahamas.

Beyond the military assistance, the Dominican government received contingents of police officers from Trinidad, Barbados, Grenada, St Lucia and Jamaica to reinforce the beleaguered Royal Dominica Police Force (RDPF). Grenada additionally despatched a team from its police Special Services Unit which joined a team of communication and logistics personnel who were sent to assist the CARICOM Disaster Relief Unit. In addition, St Lucia sent fire service personnel specialising in urban search and rescue as well as disaster assessment officials.[16] CDEMA played a pivotal role in assessing Dominica's needs and requesting appropriate assistance. The military effort, however, was coordinated through the RSS and this gives an idea of the immense value of the regional militaries, not as combat forces, but as disciplined agencies able to deploy forces for humanitarian efforts.

THE REGIONAL MILITARY AID EFFORT

Jamaica

The Jamaica Defence Force (JDF) despatched a dedicated 120-man strong Disaster Assistance Response Team (DART). Elements of the DART are still deployed in Dominica and tasked with:

- the security and distribution of relief supplies
- the provision of limited medical care
- basic engineering work with light tools and equipment (inclusive of debris removal and construction of improvised shelters)
- logistics management
- conducting damage assessments
- recovery planning [17]

The JDF provided additional assistance by detaching one of its two Damen SPa 4207 patrol vessels (the largest in its fleet) to assist the Dominica Coast Guard. The HMJS *Middlesex* conducted extensive patrols around the Dominica coast and was successful in intercepting and apprehending illegal migrants in addition to seizing illegal weapons.[18]

Barbados

The Barbados Defence Force used the Damen SPa 4207 vessels HMBS *Leonard C. Banfield* and the HMBS *Rudyard Lewis* to ferry relief supplies and personnel from the defence force and the

Barbados fire service to Dominica. The two vessels made repeated trips, evacuating casualties, transporting supplies and ferrying medical and disaster management specialists to Dominica.[19]

Trinidad and Tobago

The Trinidad and Tobago Defence Force (TTDF), aided by the National Helicopter Services Limited (NHSL) provided the largest material contribution to the initial relief effort. Two S-76 helicopters from NHSL provided critical support for transporting emergency personnel and assessment teams to remote villages to survey damage, evacuate the injured and stranded, and to deliver emergency supplies.

The Trinidad and Tobago Coast Guard deployed no fewer than three vessels to the Dominica relief effort. The first vessel was the Damen SPa 5009 vessel TTS *Moruga* which transported food, water, generators and a 21-member disaster relief team which assisted in securing and managing the distribution of relief items.[20] Additional TTDF personnel were despatched by civilian aircraft along with medical teams. Subsequently the Damen FCS 5009 TTS *Brighton* was despatched with 23.3 tonnes of relief supplies. In addition to the crew, a team from the Trinidad and Tobago Regiment along with five civilian medical personnel were also aboard to provide additional medical services and assist in relief distribution.[21] Soldiers from the Trinidad and Tobago Regiment were deployed alongside the CDPF to control the orgy of looting that followed the disaster. Finally, on 23 October 2017, the largest patrol vessel in any CARICOM Coast Guard, the TTS *Nelson* departed Port of Spain, headed for Dominica to provide further disaster relief.[22]

Bahamas

Arriving somewhat later than the other Caribbean coast guard vessels, the Royal Bahamas Defence Force vessel HMBS *Lawrence Major*, a Damen 5612 landing craft, reached Dominica on 29 October. This vessel is the only landing craft operated by CARICOM Coast Guards and has specialised disaster management packages. One of these, a mobile galley, can prepare up to 1,000 meals per day, marking a substantial improvement in the facilities available, as shown by photographs of TTDF and JDF personnel trying to cook under makeshift sheds. The HMBS *Lawrence Major* has a carrying capacity of approximately fourteen 40ft containers or twenty-eight 20ft containers of equipment and supplies. The vessel can also transport 50,000 gallons of potable water and 22,000 gallons of fuel, making it a vital asset to the relief effort.[23]

This display of regional coordination and solidarity amply showed the ability of the RSS to coordinate a substantial humanitarian relief effort and speaks well of the ability of the CARICOM countries to support each other in times of crisis. Within the constraints of limited resources, the nations of the English-speaking Caribbean have developed sufficient capabilities to take care of most minor security needs.

Arms Sales, Suppliers and Trends

The English-speaking Caribbean started out as being almost entirely equipped with weapons, vehicles and equipment supplied directly or indirectly from the British Commonwealth. The standard rifle of the region's militaries, for example, was the 7.62mm SLR, many of which were supplied from Australia. Trinidad's first armoured vehicles were Australian Dingos while the Commonwealth supplied Jamaica with many of its initial weapons, aircraft and vessels. This laid a solid tradition of mutual training, exercises and, for a brief period, even leadership from the British Commonwealth. This ended in the 1970s when the last of the seconded officers left.

The United States then emerged as a major influence in the 1980s but, even then, it took some years before it replaced the British Commonwealth as a weapons supplier. Even then, it was only in the mid-1990s when former United States Coast Guard (USCG) cutters and surplus light aircraft began to arrive in some numbers. Jamaica, in the 1970s, did take delivery of US armoured personnel carriers (APCs) to deal with internal unrest but in the main it was not until the twenty-first century that the United States began to provide equipment to the land forces of the region.

Trinidad and Tobago followed its own path and managed to re-equip most of its military with Israeli small arms with minor accretions from the United States and Germany. However, Guyana, with its 28-year flirtation with a quasi-Marxist dictatorship, procured weapons from Cuba, North Korea, the People's Republic of China, Brazil and the former Soviet Union. Unique among the countries of the English-speaking Caribbean, Guyana's military still uses Soviet-bloc weapons in some quantity despite the decline of that country's armed forces in numerical strength and importance. Guyana was also unique in obtaining field artillery in some quantity from its communist suppliers though these are largely out of service.

China's Foray

A new supplier has emerged, however, the PRC. China's push for influence among the Caribbean political elite has been replicated with an equally determined effort to court the military and the bureaucratic elite in the region, often deftly stepping in to take advantage of senseless overreactions on the part of the US, such as the suspension of military aid to Barbados after it refused to sign a Bilateral Immunity Agreement (BIA), which in turn led Barbados to avail itself of China's offer of military training and assistance.[24] The end result is that China's military training establishments now annually host a substantial number of officers from the region with an attendant increase in influence over their military leadership with a discernible shift in attitudes.

China's foray into the region's military market was initially in the form of non-lethal aid: uniforms, medical supplies, hospital equipment, engineering equipment and an extensive package of training at Chinese military academies for staff officers. This was combined with visits by a Chinese hospital ship *Peace Ark* in 2011 in a successful exercise of Beijing's soft power. The impact of these initiatives, in particular the training at Chinese academies, should not be underestimated as several officers who attended such schools have attained positions of some power and influence in their respective countries. This has also been synchronised with China's expanding economic footprint in the region. Its trade with the Latin America-Caribbean region rose to US$ 289 billion in 2013 from only US$ 12 billion in 2000 and it has also offered to invest over US$ 250 billion in the coming years.

China has not been averse to using its influence to subvert normal tendering and procurement processes, relying on courting leaders to secure arms deals. President Xi's visit to Trinidad was followed by a reciprocal visit by Prime Minister Persad-Bissessar to Beijing in February 2014, when, in a major breakthrough for Chinese arms sales to the region, the controversial purchase of a long-range maritime patrol vessel was agreed upon.[25] This was again a demonstration of the growing Chinese influence over the governments of the region, which so far had been firmly under the largely benevolent gaze and geopolitical sway of the US. The decision to buy the Chinese patrol vessel also marked the first sale of non-Western military hardware to the Caribbean nation since the end of the Cold War.[26] The purchase of this vessel was apparently tied to a loan of US$ 5 billion being offered by China to Trinidad. Similarly, the Chinese company Huawei was awarded a contract to build a national command centre without going through the stipulated tender process. The Bahamas also received two armoured vehicles and a large quantity of riot control equipment from China, again without any apparent security requirement.

Naval Vessels, Dutch Domination and Australian Influence[27]

One supplier, the Netherlands, appears to have achieved a stranglehold on Caribbean coast guards. Through Damen Shipyards Group, in ten years, from 2006 to 2016, the coast guards of Jamaica, Barbados, the Bahamas and Trinidad and Tobago have been virtually totally re-equipped with Damen patrol vessels in the 30m to 50m length range. Not only has Damen supplanted the more traditional American and British suppliers of naval vessels to these countries, it has also forged strong partnerships with the users of their products within the region – to the extent of refitting the *Nassau* and her sister-ship HMBS *Bahamas* (P-60) though they were not Dutch made, as well as building support facilities for their vessels to enable maintenance and overhaul work to be done within the region.

It is not just the Commonwealth Caribbean that has proven to be a ready market for Damen products – the coast guards of Canada, Mexico, Honduras, Ecuador, Venezuela and the United States have made large purchases of Damen designed vessels, although in the cases of the United States, Canada and Mexico, the vessels are locally made. Of these ships, the US Coast Guard Sentinel-class Fast Response Cutter (SPa 4708), with 58 being planned for induction, marks the largest class of coastal patrol vessel in the entire Western Hemisphere. To facilitate the sheer number of vessels, Damen has entered into a partnership with the Bollinger shipyard based in Louisiana.

The popularity of Damen vessels in the region is surprising considering the decidedly modest capabilities of the basic vessels. Building to standard designs (known as Standard Patrol or SPa), Damen's construction process enables vessels to be fabricated in virtual kit form and assembled and integrated in a relatively short space of time. The SPa sub-types are differentiated by their length and width – an SPa 4207 being 42m long and 7m wide, with an SPa 5009 being 50m long and 9m wide. Of the various sub-types, the SPa 4207 is used by the largest number of countries though the 5009 is gaining in popularity. A list of the countries in the English-speaking Caribbean operating Damen vessels is shown in Table 2.

The capabilities offered by the SPa vessels in their basic form are modest – the vessels are unarmed, do not come with a particularly substantial surveillance suite and have a performance that is at best barely adequate for their envisaged roles. This means that the cost per vessel can, for basic ships, be quite reasonable for coast guards on limited budgets with a basic SPa 4207 costing approximately US$ 15 million and a basic SPa 5009 coming in at US$ 23 million. The addition of armament and surveillance systems can dramatically – and at times excessively – increase the price of the vessels.

Damen's ability to break into this market and then to dominate it is largely due to its ability to deliver craft quickly at reasonable prices. Speed of delivery cannot be understated as Caribbean coast guards have a penchant for waiting until their fleets are almost on the verge of total collapse before placing fresh orders. Damen calculated that Caribbean coast guards were principally constabulary forces that did not require sophisticated naval vessels for their stipulated tasks. To this end, it was able to market its SPa vessels as cost-effective solutions to national requirements.

Table 2: Countries in the English-speaking Caribbean operating Damen vessels			
Nation	**Date**	**Quantity**	**SPa Sub-type**
Jamaica	2005	3	Two 4207 and one FCS 5009 (two 4207 and one FCS 5009 on order)
St Vincent and the Grenadines		1	4207
Barbados	2007	5	Three 4207 and two Damen 1204
Trinidad and Tobago	2015	Six (and six DI 1102 interceptors)	5009 (four SPa and two FCS)
Bahamas	2013	9	Four 4207, four 3007 and one 5612
Source: Damen Shipyards, Author's own research, Jane's Fighting Ships			

Australia's Foothold

It should be noted that Australia continues to be a supplier of vessels to Trinidad and Tobago. In 2008, Trinidad contracted with Austal for the purchase of six APB 30 patrol boats, each 30m long and displacing some 85 tonnes. The package included a five-year comprehensive maintenance and support services programme, which included scheduled and preventative maintenance support, unscheduled maintenance, management and performance of annual surveys and maintenance periods as well as shore-based engineering support. This did not work out as planned, as will be detailed in the appropriate chapter. Furthermore, two Cape-class patrol vessels are on order from Austal and these are due for delivery in 2021. Compared to Damen, Austal is a minor player but with its sale to Trinidad of two Cape-class vessels, there is likely to be some level of regional interest in their vessels.

Summary

The English-speaking Caribbean is thus a conglomeration of large and small island states and the continental country of Guyana. These countries, gaining independence in the 1960s and 1970s have evolved into democratic states though not without challenges. Their foreign policies and arms procurement policies have reflected a break with their colonial past and in some cases a distinct ideological shift from away from their traditional Western leanings. Each state has forged its own identity and although cooperation in the form of CARICOM is very much in evidence, the larger states of the English-speaking Caribbean adopt divergent policies based on their own interests in respect of the procurement of military hardware. The emergence of China as a potential supplier of military hardware and training adds a new dimension to the region's international relations.

In spite of their independent outlook, the countries of the region have displayed a remarkable degree of collective spirit when faced with security challenges in the region or humanitarian crises. On three occasions, coordinated through the RSS, the countries of the region were prepared to use their armed forces to act as peacekeepers, assist regional governments and to provide direct assistance where necessary.

2
THE BAHAMAS

The Commonwealth of the Bahamas is an archipelagic state, forming the Lucayan Archipelago, of more than 700 islands (40 of which are inhabited). The Bahamas gained its independence from the United Kingdom in 1973. The country is a bicameral democracy and a member of the British Commonwealth, retaining the Queen as its Head of State. The country has a population of over 330,000 and has one of the highest per capita incomes in the hemisphere – third after the United States and Canada – with an economy that relies heavily on the tourist industry and offshore finance.

Its military establishment – the Royal Bahamas Defence Force (RBDF), established on 31 March 1980 – is unique in the Caribbean in that it is an all-naval formation of some 1,600 personnel with an attached Air Wing with three aircraft and a commando unit tasked with amphibious operations.

History of the RBDF

The Royal Bahamas Police Force (RBPF), an unarmed, but weapons trained, force, was the principal security service in the country, performing internal security functions as well as operating the small coast guard until 1980. The RBDF was formed around a nucleus of two Vosper Thornycroft 103ft patrol vessels – the *Marlin* and the *Flamingo*. These vessels were armed with a single 20mm gun and two machine guns. One of these vessels, the *Flamingo*, would meet a tragic fate. Other vessels delivered in the mid-1980s to the 1990s included three Protector-class patrol vessels in 1986, four ex-USCG Cape-class vessels in 1989, seven Keith Nelson type patrol boats delivered to the RBPF between 1971 and 1977 and one landing craft delivered in 1991.[1]

The Flamingo Incident[2]

In its pursuit of an illegal fishing operation, the RBDF suffered its greatest loss to date. On 10 May 1980, HMBS *Flamingo* attempted to arrest two Cuban fishing vessels – *Ferrocem 165* and *Ferrocem 54* – operating in Bahamian waters.

The two Cuban fishing vessels were boarded and searched by an HMBS *Flamingo* boarding team, the four Cubans on each vessel were arrested and the large quantity of fish aboard the two vessels was confiscated. As such, the two vessels, *Ferrocem 165* and *Ferrocem 54*, were taken into tow and into custody by the *Flamingo*.

En route to Cay Santo Domingo, two Cuban MiG-21s 'buzzed' the Bahamian ship. In an unprovoked attack, the fighters opened fire with their 23mm guns parallel to the *Flamingo*'s starboard side and directly in front of the ship's bow. Fortunately, nobody was injured in this first strike. The Bahamian crew assumed that the display was aimed at intimidating the Bahamian vessel into releasing the captured fishermen.

Commander Rolle, Captain of the *Flamingo*, ordered his crew to hoist a second ensign and a Bahamian flag. With very clear weather conditions, it was inconceivable that the MiGs, flying at very low altitude, could be mistaken in the identity of the *Flamingo* and basic navigation would have placed the vessels well within Bahamian territorial waters. The actions that followed thereafter are thus even more bizarre and speak of a deliberate and malign intent on the part of the Cuban military.

Some 45 minutes after the first attack, MiG-21s returned with a vengeance. The *Flamingo* was less than 3km away from Cay Santo Domingo. The MiG-21s attacked the Flamingo with a combination of 23mm gunfire and 57mm rockets, severely damaging the RBDF vessel. The RBDF account notes:

> The Operations room filled with water and rendered all communication equipment down. The bridge burst into flames. Melting steel appeared all around from the rocket attack and as it was in danger of imminent sinking, the crew abandoned ship. Even as the ship sank and the crew attempted to swim to safety, the jets returned, strafing the surrounding waters with machine gun fire and tearing apart the two lifeboats that had been jettisoned overboard. Although the jets disappeared, a military helicopter remained in the area.
>
> The dory, driven by M/S Whitfield Neely, now Lieutenant Commander, who had been stationed on one of the captured craft, collected all the survivors, four of whom were wounded. Roll-call revealed that four marines-A/B Fenrick Sturrup and M/S David Tucker, Edward Williams and Austin Smith-were missing.
>
> HMBS Flamingo's crew had managed to secure a sub machine gun with one magazine of 30 rounds and a pistol before they abandoned ship. This was no match for their menacing machine

A Damen SPa 3007-class patrol vessel of the RBDF. (Damen Shipyards)

Table 3: The RBDF Today

	Total Strength	Army	Air Force	Navy
Active personnel	1,540 end 2017	400	n/k 30	1,110
Reserves	50	0	0	50

chaperone hovering above. Thankfully, the helicopter left after the *Flamingo* had completely sunk. A search of the area for the four missing men ensued, in lifeboats, to no avail. All persons were then transferred to the *Ferrocem 165* and they departed the area under the cloak of darkness to find cover at Ragged Island.

The other vessel, *Ferrocem 54* was left drifting as the engine was shot out. The remaining crew took turns smoking cigarettes as a means of light with which to navigate in a darkened ship state. This proved to be a wise decision, as the Cubans returned, in hopes of leaving no survivors and rescuing their own. The Bahamian crew and their prisoners arrived at the Bay of Anchorage at the southern tip of Ragged Island at 1330 on Sunday morning and proceeded to Duncan Town on foot. Telegraphs were sent to Nassau informing about the tragedy and bold attacks by the Cubans.[3]

Four crewmen were killed – Fenrick Sturrup, Austin Smith, David Tucker and Edward Williams – with 16 survivors being rescued by Bahamian prize crews aboard one of the two fishing vessels that they had attempted to arrest. Cuba eventually paid compensation to the tune of between US$ 4 million and 10 million, and the poachers on board its two fishing vessels were convicted. The incident makes the RBDF unique among Commonwealth Caribbean navies in that it lost a vessel to air attack.

It should be noted that from every account, the conduct of the *Flamingo*'s crew was exemplary and worthy of praise. The fact that the crew was able to secure weapons, despite the extreme situation, speaks of the credit of the discipline and training of the RBDF crew and their training and leadership.

The Royal Bahamas Defence Force (RBDF) increased its strength from approximately 1,218 personnel in 2014 to over 1,460 in 2016 – a rate of about 80 per year, with the total by 2021 exceeding 1,600. This expansion is necessary to support the ongoing procurement of additional naval vessels and expansion of shore infrastructure, specifically the establishment of three new forward operating bases.

The stated strategic mission of the Royal Bahamas Defence Force (RBDF) is to defend national sovereignty, assist with maintaining law and order, and perform humanitarian relief tasks. In practice, this means countering the trafficking of drugs, small arms, and people; combating illegal fishing; conducting search and rescue; and providing aid in the wake of tropical storms and hurricanes. The RBDF's 'army' elements are more equivalent to marines and primarily support naval units in these missions, for example by embarking on vessels to conduct visit, board, search, and seizure tasks. However, the RBDF also carries out security operations on land, including in support of the national police, but has to date not been called upon to perform any particularly challenging internal security operations, with their greatest challenges coming in the aftermath of hurricanes which often occasion an orgy of looting beyond the scope of the local police to handle effectively. The RBDF is not currently configured for any type of major combat operations.

Training for the RBDF Marines includes the following, as described by the RBDF:

1) A Militarization Phase:
This is the Initial Indoctrination for enlistment training. It comprises of ten (10) subject areas fused with elementary physical fitness. The duration of this phase is five (5) weeks. In week 3 recruits will engage in a progress exam in academics and elementary fitness. Week 4 a Demerit and Disciplinary System is activated comprised of a variety of different classes of offences (infractions) and consequences. In addition a merit worth and value system is outlined for outstanding performance. New Entry Training also inspires leadership through a dynamic leadership model to develop the military aptitude and leadership skills of recruits. In week (5) five final examinations for the phase are executed. Exams are IT based and are generated discretely per recruit. Recruits who fail exams will receive a warning letter to encourage successful completion. If successful with the re-sits, the recruit will transition to the next phase.

2) A Maritime Phase:
The maritime phase of the New Entry Training will comprise of ten (10) nautical science subjects including Advanced Drills, Intermediate Physical Fitness, Advanced Drills (weapon) and an Initial Sea Training Exercise. In week 8 progress exams are conducted to confirm learning objectives. Week 9 is an Initial Sea Training Exercise designed to ensure that the theoretical concepts delivered are practically conceptualized within a dynamic maritime

A Damen Spa 4207-class patrol boat. (Damen Shipyards)

Three RBDF vessels in port, including (from left to right), Damen 5612, Bahamas-class OPV, and Damen 4207. (Damen Shipyards)

Another view of the same three vessels, offering a better look at details of their superstructures and equipment. (Damen Shipyards)

environment. In week 10 recruits will engage in final assessments for the phase. Successful recruits will transition to phase 3. Unsuccessful recruits will receive warning letters and will have to successfully complete re-sits. Failure of re-sits, may result in a recruit being back-phased or dismissed from New Training.

3) A Naval Infantry Phase:
This is a four week competency based phase comprising of ten (10) infantry professional subjects. Recruits will have to demonstrate understanding of theoretical concepts within practical combat training exercises in an amphibious (land and maritime) environment. Recruits will engage in intermediate weapons training, combat conditioning, patrolling, self-defence training, medical and combat communications training in conjunction with waterborne combat techniques. Successful recruits will receive Infantry Certification. Those who perform admirably will be sited for additional infantry training. Recruits who are unsuccessful will have an opportunity to complete a re-sit in order to receive the Infantry Certification.

4) A Final Phase:
This phase involves additional training for STCW and First Responders certification, trafficking in Persons awareness training, Financial planning, and Defence Force Departmental Introductions and Partner Agencies acquaint. Preparations for the New Entry Passing Out Parade is finalized.

Defence Force recruits are also indoctrinated into the importance of discipline and character development through a core value system that sets the standard for the organization's military culture. This against a background of a rigorous physical fitness program challenges potential marines into a career that demands respect, commitment and devotion to duty for God and country.[4]

Land Forces

The RBDF's primary land combat element is the Commando Squadron,[5] which is at least the size of a reinforced company with a strength of some 150 personnel. Although equipped with only light weapons and reliant on Land Rover tactical vehicles, the force is fairly competent, benefiting from routine training with US marines and the Rhode Island National Guard, and other support from the United States. Its infantry weapons seem to be a mix of US M16/M4 platforms and IMI Galils as the standard assault rifle with the FN MAG as the standard machine gun at section and platoon level. The Uzi submachine gun has also been observed in service while older weapons such as the Sterling L2A3 submachine gun and the L1A1 SLR are held as reserve weapons or for ceremonial purposes. It should also be noted that RBDF Marines are issued with shotguns for maritime boarding operations.

The Commando Squadron draws its strength from RBDF Marines who then undergo specialised training, detailed by the RBDF:

> Selected Commando Squadron marines receive training in a number of professional military subjects in areas such as Counterterrorism, Amphibious Operations, Demolition and Explosives Identification and Recognition, Skill at Arms, Communications, and Field Craft. They also participate in the marine phase of Trade Winds, an annual exercise that includes

forces from the Caribbean, the United Kingdom, and the United States.[6]

Two armoured vehicles were delivered from China in May 2017.[7] These were Tiger 4x4 APCs fitted with a turret and smoke grenade dischargers but lacked armament. The majority of the unit is based at HMBS Coral Harbour, although it has detachments at the RBDF's other facilities in order to properly support naval operations. The squadron is capable of conducting conventional infantry operations but is also trained to undertake counterterrorism, amphibious, and maritime security operations. The Commando Squadron also has personnel with specialised skills such as explosive ordnance disposal. China supplied two 38mm grenade launchers, 10,038 tear gas and smoke grenade launchers and 60 sets of night vision goggles in addition to the two Tiger APCs.[8]

The RBDF also has a Military Police Force Protection Unit that provides security for military facilities, civilian ports, prisons, and other government facilities. The force also supports and undertakes joint operations with the Royal Bahamas Police Force, as well as the customs and immigration departments. In addition, the RBDF has an elite Special Operations Unit, although information on this force is understandably scarce. Given the relatively benign threat environment in the Bahamas, these forces are sufficient. It should also be noted that compared to countries such as Guyana, Jamaica and Trinidad and Tobago, the Bahamas does not have as serious a problem with violent crime or with heavily armed street gangs challenging the authority of the state. This enables the Bahamas to concentrate on naval forces.

The RBDF Naval Forces

The naval orientation of the RBDF stands in stark contrast to the army dominated establishments that are to be found in other islands, at times to the detriment of the naval element – as in the case of Jamaica. It may be that with the Royal Bahamas Police Force (RBPF) of over 4,000 members being deemed sufficient for internal security functions, the RBDF has been allowed to concentrate on the maritime domain from which most of the country's security challenges – narcotics, illegal fishing, poaching and illegal immigration being chief among them – emanate.

The RBDF Fleet Today[9]

As might be expected the RBDF has always maintained a sizeable naval fleet (by regional standards) with pride of place being given to two 60m OPVs – HMBS *Bahamas* (P60) and HMBS *Nassau* (P61). Other major, but badly ageing, assets include the 108 ft HMBS *Yellow Elder* (P03) – the last of three Protector-class patrol vessels, four cutters in the 40ft to 50ft size range and a number of inshore patrol craft. In addition, the sole survivor of a class of five 60ft patrol boats HMBS *Inagua* (P27) is still nominally on strength, though of dubious value even when new.

The RBDF faced a number of materiel and manpower challenges as its surface assets aged, suppliers and original equipment manufacturers of older equipment went out of business or changed hands and, rather more seriously, a problem of recruiting quality personnel. On 5 December 2006, the then RBDF Commander described a pathetic state of affairs in which only two vessels were seaworthy, there was no pilot for the single operational aircraft and revealed that up to 25 percent of RBDF personnel were what he termed 'bad apples'. To its credit, the RBDF embarked upon a major overhaul of its system, with the results being seen from 2008 onwards. By reducing personnel strength by up to a third, the RBDF was able to rid itself of many undesirable people and made significant strides in restoring its fleet, vehicles and air assets to operational status. This had a tangible impact as narcotics seizures increased substantially.[10]

Despite its efforts to keep existing assets serviceable, it became clear to the RBDF that a major force recapitalisation programme was needed. To this end, it initiated the Sandy Bottom Project which at US$ 232 million is the largest capital investment made by the RBDF since its inception. This project entails the construction of new naval bases, the dredging of harbours and the development of ports. In addition, the complete re-equipment of the RBDF surface fleet is being undertaken which, upon completion, will result in the RBDF having adequate numbers of modern patrol craft to conduct operations within its maritime domain.

Table 4: RBDF Vessels

Class	Pennant Number	Ship	Commissioned
Bahamas-class	P 60	*Bahamas*	12 January 1999 Being refitted at a Bahamian shipyard with assistance from Damen
	P 61	*Nassau*	12 January 1999 Sent to Damen in August 2016 – to be returned to service within 9 months
Damen Stan 4207	P 421	*Arthur Dion Hanna*	22 June 2014
	P 422	*Durward Knowles*	31 July 2014
	P 423	*Leon Livingstone Smith*	22 September 2014
	P 424	*Rolly Gray*	30 April 2015
Damen Stan 3007	P 301	*Lignum Vitae*	March 2015
	P 302	*Cascarilla*	March 2016
	P 303	*Kamalame*	Late 2016
	P 304	*Madeira*	Late 2016
Damen Stan Lander 5612	A01	*Lawrence W. Major*	March 2016

A SPa 4207-lass HMBS *Durward Knowles* of the RBDF. (Damen Shipyards)

A Damen 5612-class HMBS *Lawrence Major* landing ship. (Damen Shipyards)

Being undertaken by the Dutch companies of Van Oord (for infrastructure) and Damen (for surface assets), the Sandy Bottom Project will enable the RBDF to implement its decentralisation programme over the next few years. With a programme that includes the development of RBDF bases at strategic locations in the northern, central and southern regions of the Lucayan Archipelago, enabling the dispersed deployment of personnel, ships and aircraft, it is envisaged that this strategy will also enable the RBDF to provide coverage of the country's maritime domain in the fight against illegal migration, poaching of marine resources, arms smuggling, illicit narcotics, human trafficking and potential terrorist related activities. Given the fact that the Bahamas has experienced severe damage from hurricanes, it is hoped that the decentralisation strategy will also enhance the RBDF's overall efficiency in conducting search and rescue and disaster relief operations. Indeed, as an archipelagic state, the pressures on the RBDF to conduct such operations in a timely and efficacious manner cannot be overstated.

While the infrastructural works are still in progress, three RBDF bases have new dredging and infrastructural development, which were completed by the end of 2016. These are the RBDF headquarters at Coral Harbour in New Providence Island, Matthew Town in Great Inagua Island, and the Gun Point base in Ragged Island. Headway has also been made in acquiring new surface assets; Damen has supplied four Stan Patrol 4207 patrol vessels, four Stan Patrol 3007 patrol vessels and one Stan Lander 5612 landing craft. Damen also completely overhauled and returned to service HMBS *Bahamas* and HMBS *Nassau* in 2017.[11]

While these vessels are not particularly well-equipped and lack modern surveillance equipment and weapons (only the *Bahamas* and *Nassau* are armed with anything more than machine guns), these ships are adequate to the patrol and constabulary tasks assigned to them and represent a cost-effective solution.[12]

The acquisition of the Damen Stan Lander is of particular note as its primary function is to assist in disaster relief operations and to this end, comes with containerised disaster relief packages which includes a 17-piece mobile base – locally termed the 'Mobile Base City'. These resources have been deployed to assist the community of North Andros which had suffered significant damage from Hurricane Matthew in October 2016.[13] Unique among the islands of the English-speaking Caribbean, the Bahamas has maintained a landing craft of naval strength since 1991 and is indicative of its desire for effective amphibious landing capabilities.

Air Assets

The RBDF Air Wing was formed on 26 November 1981. Its initial assets were three Aero Commanders purchased from Bahamasair and operated by the RBDF. These were sold off in 1990. In 1992, the RBDF procured a Cessna 402 and shortly thereafter a Cessna 421 followed. These two aircraft were phased out in the early 2000s when, in 2005, the delivery of a Super King Air 350 took place, followed in May 2009 by a Cessna 208 Turbine Caravan with floats and a Partenavia P.68 which dramatically improved the RBDF's surveillance and transport capabilities.[14]

In December 2019, Bahamas established the Bahamas Unmanned Aerial System programme. Under this programme Swift Engineering has been contracted to provide 55 unmanned aerial vehicles.

With its modernisation plan, well underway and making good progress, the capability of the RBDF will be significantly boosted and it can be expected to make a greater contribution to the country's

Table 5: RBDF Air Assets

Type	Quantity	Service	Example Serials
Aero Commander 500S	3	1976–1990	C6-BEP, C6-DBF, C6-BEM
Cessna 421	1	1988–2002	DF-1001/A
Cessna 404	1	1991–2008	DF-1002/B
Piper PA-31 Navajo	2	1993–present	RBDF1-2
Beech King Air 350	1	2005–present	C6-BDF
Cessna 208 Caravan	1	2007–present	C6-AWO
Partenavia P-68C Observer	1	2009–present	C6-CDF

safety. However, it is noteworthy that the RBDF's Air Wing which comprises single examples of the Beech King Air and the Cessna 208 has received little attention. Given the geographical realities of the country, it is surprising that no priority has yet been given to either expanding or modernising this inadequate force. It is hoped that this will assume a greater degree of urgency in the near future.

The RBDF Air Wing has only three aircraft: a King Air 350, Vulcanair/Partenavia P68C, and Cessna 208B Grand Caravan. The small number means that they are by necessity multipurpose aircraft, being tasked to perform reconnaissance, search and rescue, medical evacuation, transport, and other duties. The small fleet also means that comprehensive coverage of all Bahamian air space is not possible and availability of aircraft to support operations is not assured, especially without specialised surveillance sensors.

A view of the loading area of the HMBS *Lawrence Major*. (via author)

There do not seem to be any current plans to expand the Air Wing although the RBDF would benefit from additional assets to support surface ships in interdiction missions. The RBDF also recognises that helicopters would be useful for surveillance and other operations, but these have been deemed too expansive to procure. That said, the government has reported that a programme to acquire unmanned aerial vehicles is underway, although it is unclear how long it will take to deliver a capability. However, in 2016, a live aerial drone training exercise was undertaken and the development of a UAV unit is in progress with 55 short and medium range drones on order.[15] The order is to be broken up as follows and covers all security agencies:

> 55 drones (with the start-up number to cover all MONS agencies for the first year)
> - 6 Short Range UAVs (Main UAS stations throughout the country)
> - 24 Close Range UAVs with vertical take-off or catapult launch/net retrieval that can be used on RBDF craft and in the field with options for water retrieval if failure occurs (RBDF, Police, Immigration)
> - 20 Very Low Cost Close Range UAVs that have a range of 10km, endurance time of 20 to 45 minutes and underwater capability options (Police, Customs and Immigration)
> - 5 Tethered Drones for use at Bahamas Department of Corrections (HMP and coastal outpost stations on the island of New Providence[16]

Disaster Relief

All armed forces in the English-speaking Caribbean have performed creditably in disaster relief operations. However, the unique geographical position of the Bahamas means that, again perhaps unique among the armed forces of the CARICOM nations, it has a published and publicised list of functions for the hurricane season which lasts from 1 June to 30 November each year. Its stated position is that:

> Prior to a hurricane, the Royal Bahamas Defence Force is tasked with the following duties:
> - The securing and security of HMBS Coral Harbour, RBDF ships, RBDF aircrafts, Northern and Southern Command Satellite Bases, and outpost sites such as Government House and the Detention Center.
> - To help in securing homes of families of RBDF members deployed overseas and those listed as 'missing at sea'.
> - To provide disaster relief assistance to islands affected post hurricane.
> - To conduct search and rescue as necessary, with care taken to the prevailing circumstances and conditions.

Bahamas-class OPV on initial trials after refit. (Damen Shipyards)

> Thirty-six hours before a hurricane is predicted to make landfall, a twelve-member team of the Royal Bahamas Defence Force is dispatched to the National Emergency Management Agency (NEMA) Operation Center. This team is comprised of one Officer, who acts as liaison officer between the RBDF and other agencies, two Petty Officers, six Leading Hands, and three Able Hands. The Marines are tasked with various responsibilities such as recording unofficial reports of damages to various islands during and after the storm has passed. They are also responsible for the charting and tracking of the storm as well as keeping various state board up to date.
>
> A team of marines comprised of the Advanced Support Team is also deployed to islands which may be impacted by the hurricane. They assist local authorities and communities on these islands.[17]

When Hurricane Dorian hit the Bahamas in September 2019, the RBDF sent its vessels to safety in the United States, returning only when the storm had passed. The relief effort, until the return of the RBDF's ships, was borne by the land based RBDF elements alongside the officers of the Royal Bahamas Police Force. The scale of the devastation, however, overwhelmed the RBDF and the Bahamian authorities.

Despite the deployment of the Commando Squadron and the country's two APCs, residents complained bitterly that the RBDF and RBPF failed to provide adequate security from looters. Indeed, the entire response of the Bahamian government was widely, if at times unfairly, criticised. The fact is that the RBDF deployed almost its full strength to the effort but found itself totally overwhelmed. The scale of the RBDF's deployment:

> The RBDF, despite deploying nearly all of its assets, including its commando squadron with two Chinese-made Tiger APCs, has come under severe criticism for its failure to stop the orgy of looting and violence that has followed the aftermath of the hurricane. In addition, its failure to charter or coordinate with civilian aircraft and boats to maximize the relief effort has been severely criticized … The RBDF has deployed its force of two Bahamas-class 60m OPVs, Damen Stan Patrol 4207 and 3007 vessels, plus the Damen Stan Lander HMBS Lawrence Major to reach the affected people and its survey flight has conducted extensive aerial reconnaissance. The HMBS Lawrence Major has containerized disaster relief modules which can be deployed to provide medical, catering and basic sanitation facilities to disaster victims. However, the force has only three light aircraft and no helicopters.[18]

The challenges faced by the RBDF in the aftermath of Hurricane Dorian are symptomatic of the problems confronting the armed

A Tiger APC of the RBDF. (Mark Lepko Collection)

Bahamas-class HMBS *Nassau* of the RBDF. (Damen Shipyards)

forces of the region when faced with major calamities. Law and order collapses all too often when a disaster occurs, placing additional pressure on already beleaguered police and military personnel. In this respect, the RBDF was bound to be criticised but it is difficult to fault the scale of their response to the unprecedented natural disaster.

Conclusion

The naval orientation of the RBDF is unique among the countries of the English-speaking Caribbean. However, the Bahamas maintains an adequate force of personnel capable of conducting internal security operations on land and this force, supported by the Commando Squadron is well-trained and reasonably well-equipped. However, as was seen by the experience of Hurricane Dorian, the RBDF can be overwhelmed by the scale of a calamity and its resources stretched to its limits.

The RBDF Coast Guard is well-equipped with modern vessels, and though these lack advanced surveillance equipment, their availability, in quantity and at a reasonably high level of serviceability, means that the Bahamas has adequate means to patrol its maritime domain and ensure its security against minor threats such as narcotics smuggling and poaching.

However, the RBDF remains severely deficient in air support with the three aircraft available to the force being wholly inadequate to perform the requisite surveillance of the archipelago. While the aircraft have some limited utility as transports, their limited payload and range make them suitable for liaison and transport of low volume cargo. This has proved to be an issue during natural disasters when the country has had to seek assistance from regional powers with larger transport aircraft. The lack of any helicopter assets is also somewhat peculiar given the inherent versatility of such aircraft and their evident military utility.

Nevertheless, the RBDF, for its size and orientation, is a professional and reasonably capable outfit that can perform its stated functions with a degree of efficacy. Given the security challenges facing the Bahamas, mainly relating to organised crime, smuggling and illegal fishing, the RBDF seems to be positioning itself to be able to confront these challenges for the foreseeable future. It should be noted, that among all the CARICOM countries, the RBDF is unique in pursuing a UAV programme for surveillance duties. This would plug many of the surveillance gaps now plaguing the RBDF and will enhance its overall effectiveness.

3

THE ARMED FORCES OF BARBADOS

Barbados is perhaps unique among the smaller armed forces of the region in attempting to conduct operations well above those its resources would otherwise permit. It houses the Regional Security System's CLO as well as maintaining a coordination role for the security of the smaller states of the Eastern Caribbean, all of whom lack any meaningful military capabilities. Furthermore, Barbados has often played a major role in more robust operations within the region as in their small but important role in Urgent Fury and in the coordination of a regional response to the 1990 coup in Trinidad.

History

The Barbados Defence Force can trace its history to the Barbados Volunteer Force (BVF) of 1902 and the colony of Barbados contributed troops to the West India Regiment (WIR) in the two world wars. In 1948, the BVF was, following the disbanding of the West India Regiment, re-established and renamed the Barbados Regiment, receiving its first colours in 1953. In the years 1959 and 1962, Barbados was part of the West Indies Federation. In this capacity, Barbados contributed the lion's share of the troops intended to form the 3rd Battalion, West India Regiment. However, on the break-up of the Federation, and the emergence of Barbados as an independent nation, the Barbados Regiment once again received its colours but was not reactivated as a military unit for many years, performing as a ceremonial unit with minimal military potential, though it was deployed in the aftermath of Hurricane Janet in 1955 and again in 1966 when the RBPF lost control of crowds during the country's independence celebrations, which turned rather unruly and somewhat violent.[1]

Once the country gained independence in 1966, Barbados was in no hurry to create a separate military. The RBPF was deemed to be adequate to deal with internal security. The RBPF was an unarmed force though its personnel received weapons training and the force held a stockpile of small arms for use in emergencies. The RBPF's weapons, however, were at best antiquated and, as became evident during the 1983 peacekeeping operation in Grenada, the main weapon available to the RBPF was the 0.303 Rifle No.4 Mk.1 which was used to arm the force of RBPF personnel sent to Grenada. It was evident from the mid-1970s, that the RBPF was not going to be capable of providing an adequate internal security force for the island. In this respect, the experience of the RBPF mirrored that of many Caribbean police forces. Like the police forces of most Caribbean islands that were former British colonies, the RBPF personnel received weapons training but were not usually issued with firearms and, even when issued, there were strict rules on the employment of such weapons during law enforcement operations. This proved to be quite adequate for the first decade's post-independence and a relatively stable internal situation militated against any idea of immediately establishing a military force in Barbados that was more than a token military entity.

Some years later, however, it was realised that a more robust force was needed in light of a somewhat volatile regional environment, and the first steps towards creating a military took place when a coast guard was formed in 1974 as the Barbados Coast Guard Civilian Unit Service. Despite its name, it was tasked with maritime constabulary functions and as such found itself requiring small arms. It was not until 1979, however, that Barbados finally took the step to establish the Barbados Defence Force as a military unit, with land and maritime elements and sanctioned through legislation. This was not without controversy and was in many ways forced out of necessity.[2]

Political Imperatives for Forming the BDF

The BDF was formed, at least in part, out of the regional political situation which saw, in October 1976, two separate incidents. One involved the bizarre incident of a Barbadian national, resident overseas, by the name of Sidney Burnett-Alleyne, who was intercepted off the coast of Martinique, apparently planning to overthrow the Barbadian government. The second incident, on 6 October, saw the destruction of a Cuban airliner after its departure from the international airport in Barbados. Three years later, the revolution in Grenada, which ousted the despotic Prime Minister Eric Gairy in favour of the Marxist New JEWEL government of Maurice Bishop, posed an apparent threat to democratic states in the region.[3] Although there was no immediate threat of communist insurrection in any of the other countries of the English-speaking Caribbean, the spectre of Bishop's success, his charisma and the appeal of his revolutionary rhetoric gave cause for concern among the more staid, conservative, Afro-Saxon leaders of the region, especially given Cuba's open support for the Grenadian revolution and the rapid build-up and expansion of that country's armed forces.

This reinforced the view of the Barbadian leadership, then under the Barbados Labour Party led by Tom Adams, that the creation of the BDF was the correct step and was needed to provide improved security for the island. This became ever more necessary since Sidney Burnett-Alleyne made no secret of his intention to continue to try to overthrow the government of Barbados and declare himself 'archduke' of the country![4] Burnett-Alleyne's threats, as comical as they might seem, were to be taken seriously as he was a known arms smuggler and was able to interact with mercenaries. To that extent, Burnett-Alleyne was deemed to pose a real danger to an island like Barbados, which, during his initial coup-plotting attempts, did not have a military of any significance with which to oppose an armed attempt to oust a government. Grenada proved that a small force of insurgents, with a reasonable level of organisation, could overthrow a government, despite the latter having an armed police force at its disposal, without undue difficulty.

The BDF – Formation and Policy Orientation

The BDF, small as it was with only a sub-strength infantry battalion with five sub-units, was soon being used in action as an element of Barbadian foreign policy. The BDF initially included an administrative 'squadron', an infantry element, also then termed a 'squadron', the Barbados Regiment (for ceremonial purposes), a pioneer squadron (for engineering purposes) and the Barbados Coast Guard.[5] The force was small, not particularly well-equipped – using a mixture of vintage weapons and more up to date NATO standard rifles and machine guns – and had limited transport resources and next to no useable air support, being dependent on civilian aircraft. Its deployment on overseas operations, therefore, was more for prestige than practical effect.

The Formation of the Barbados Coast Guard

As indicated earlier, the Barbados Coast Guard Service was established as a civilian unit in August 1974 and initially located at Enterprise, Christ Church. As a civilian service, the roles of the Coast Guard Service during this civilian period were limited to search and rescue, and investigating the illegal entry of people and goods, while enforcing the law against the dynamiting of fish around the coastal waters of Barbados.

This civilian service, known as the Coast Guard Civilian Unit Service, served for over four years but was finally dissolved in September 1978. With the decision being taken to create a Barbados Defence Force, the coast guard was briefly known as the Maritime Wing of the Barbados Regiment. However, the Defence Act of 1979 (Part X) created the legislative framework needed for the creation of the Barbados Coast Guard to serve as the maritime element of the new Barbados Defence Force. Under the Defence Act, the Coast Guard now has expanded roles and responsibilities and is now formally an armed service, subject to military discipline and rules. The shift from a civilian agency to a militarised entity has allowed for improved equipment and armed vessels.[6]

By the 1980s, the Barbados Coast Guard had some 125 personnel, a strength it maintained into the mid-1990s. Its largest asset until it was decommissioned and scuttled in 2016, was the *Trident* a 37.5m British built patrol boat that entered service in 1981. This vessel, equipped with a 40mm gun (later replaced by a 20mm weapon), was the largest vessel in the Barbados Coast Guard, supplemented by six other vessels. These included one 30-tonne Guardian-class vessel (from a total of three acquired in the 1970s), an 11.5-tonne Lewis-class vessel – also British built – and two converted shrimp boats.[7] The Barbados Coast Guard was not a recipient of the gifts of Point-class cutters that the United States gave to several Caribbean islands – Trinidad and Tobago and Jamaica being recipients of four such vessels and two vessels respectively. This meant that the

Table 6: Barbados Defence Force Air Wing				
Aircraft Type	**Quantity**	**Service Entry**	**Out of Service**	**Origin**
Beech 65 Queen Air	1	1979	1981	leased
Cessna 402C Utiliner	1	1981	1985	USA

Barbados Coast Guard remained, throughout much of its early life, indeed until 2008, a force dependent on the *Trident* with limited support from smaller vessels which were themselves of very dubious capability.

The Barbados Defence Force Air Wing

Barbados established a security Air Wing in 1971 but shortly after its formation in 1979, the BDF created an Air Wing which first operated a leased Beech Queen Air. In 1981, after the lease of the aircraft expired, the BDF obtained, and owned, a single Cessna 402. Surprisingly, this aircraft was retired in 1985 and has not been replaced to date. The lack of an Air Wing has been somewhat mitigated by the fact that the BDF is able to make use of the two C-26 Metroliners of the RSS which are both equipped for surveillance operations. However, the lack of even a light air transport capability is a lacuna that seems somewhat surprising and unusual.[8]

First Operations

Tom Adams articulated a sub-regional defence policy based on a pro-Western orientation. The so-called 'Adams Doctrine' led to the fledgling BDF being deployed to St Vincent in 1979 to quell a rebellion and were deployed twice in 1981 – once in March and again in December – to Dominica to deal with coup attempts on that island.[9] In addition to these deployments, Barbados had to be wary of a coup attempt code-named 'Operation Red Dog', also in Dominica, this time linked to the ubiquitous Sidney Burnett-Alleyne, in April 1981, which was stopped by timely intervention by the United States Bureau of Alcohol, Firearms and Tobacco (ATF).[10] That Barbados was willing to intervene in neighbouring islands was surprising, especially given the reticence of countries with larger armed forces – Trinidad and Tobago and Jamaica for example – to embark on such ventures. This tendency of Barbados to take a lead role in supporting military intervention was evident in 1983.

Urgent Fury – The BDF's Role

Though the Barbados Defence Force would only supply a single rifle platoon – which was deployed alongside a substantial contingent from the RBPF – to the Caribbean Peacekeeping Force in Grenada, its role, and that of Barbados in planning the military intervention of 1983, assisted considerably in Operation Urgent Fury. It should be noted that the main role arrogated onto itself by Barbados was that of planning and providing intelligence. Barbados was never under any illusion as to its military capacity to carry out any meaningful military operation against Grenada in 1983.

On 16 October 1983, Major Mark Adkin, a former British Army officer, was serving as staff officer of training and operations of the BDF. He was summoned to the office of Colonel Rudyard Lewis, the Chief of Staff of the BDF, and told to put together the outline of a plan to rescue Maurice Bishop, then still alive but being held captive by the Revolutionary Military Council now ruling Grenada. Adkin was told to make an assessment of troops and assets that might be required to rescue Bishop from house arrest, being further told that he should not concern himself with where the troops and equipment would come from, which was the first inkling that the United States was preparing a military operation into Grenada.[11]

To aid him in his task, Adkin was fortunate to have knowledge of Lieutenant Commander Peter Tomlin, who was the intelligence officer of the newly formed Regional Security System. Tomlin was an able naval officer and had a good knowledge of Grenada and of Maurice Bishop with whom he was personally acquainted, meeting the latter on several occasions including 14 March 1979, the day after Bishop's successful coup.[12] After the events of October 1979, and the overthrow of Bishop's government and his subsequent imprisonment, Tomlin captained a Barbados Coast Guard vessel into Grenada's St George's harbour, accompanied by a CIA operative and a Canadian representative to make an assessment of the ground situation and to explore the situation of foreign nationals who might want to escape from Grenada, a circumstance deemed likely owing to the extreme tension in the country and the prospect of significant violence. The spectre of the latter was to manifest itself less than a week later when violence erupted with tragic consequences for Bishop and several members of his cabinet along with many Grenadian civilians.

The professional skills of Adkin and the knowledge of and reconnaissance undertaken by Tomlin were augmented by the detailed knowledge of Grenada by Major Mike Hartland, a former British army officer who was serving with the Barbados Defence Force. Hartland had spent 11 years in Grenada, between 1968 and 1979, and knew the country as well as the key personalities involved in the ongoing crisis. The three officers, along with the rest of their staff, were able to create a draft plan for Bishop's rescue within a few hours of getting their instructions from Colonel Lewis.[13] This speaks volumes in respect of the professionalism of the BDF staff officers and of the value of intimate local knowledge by people familiar with the countries in question.

This plan envisaged an operation by surprise *coup de main* and anticipated a hostile reception from the Grenadian People's Revolutionary Army (PRA). The first phase would be undertaken in darkness with troops staging an airborne heliborne assault with the principal targets being Bishop's house, where he was being held under house arrest, the Governor-General's residence, the airfields at Pearls and Salines, the radio station, and the stationing of troops at a number of blocking or ambush positions to the north and south of the Grenadian capital, St Georges. The plan did not envisage engaging or attacking PRA troop concentrations but rather preventing them from intervening while Bishop was rescued. Adkin proposed that the operation would require two battalions with a third being available for deployment in the event of necessity.[14] As a rescue mission, the plan was quite realistic and it might have been quite feasible had it been approved.

The plan was received and the concept approved by Colonel Lewis who took it to Prime Minister Tom Adams but it got no further than a draft plan and no serious work was done to take the operation forward or to work towards preparing a breakdown of the force composition required to undertake this rescue mission.[15] However, Colonel Lewis and Prime Minister Adams wanted the BDF to continue to gather information and to this end, the BDF was to play a most important role in the planning for Urgent Fury, with BDF personnel and equipment being deployed in an innovative manner to maximise intelligence gathering without sophisticated surveillance equipment.

On or about 17 October, two days before Bishop's murder and the establishment of the Revolutionary Military Council, two BDF personnel – 2nd Lieutenant Alvin Quintyne and Lance Corporal Martia Browne – masqueraded as a couple on holiday and volunteered to covertly infiltrate Grenada to examine the situation and report on visible troop deployments. The two BDF soldiers, routing through St Vincent, were interrogated by officials at Pearls Airport.[16] Quintyne's knowledge of Grenada, which he had visited before, was thorough enough to convince the immigration officials at Pearls of their bona fides and the two conducted as thorough a reconnaissance as possible and noted no PRA units or anti-aircraft batteries at Pearls. They were given a lift by a Cuban truck driver who was armed with an assault rifle but otherwise noted nothing particularly untoward. However, they could not reach Salines airfield but noticed many military vehicles at Frequente. Their mission was curtailed when they discovered a man attempting to look through the door to their room.[17] Quintyne decided that the two should leave and they departed on 18 October, just one day before Grenada's descent into bloody violence which led to the beginning of the end of the Grenada Revolution and the subsequent military intervention by the United States to restore what was quaintly termed 'constitutional authority' on the island.

The single aircraft of the BDF Air Wing – the lone Cessna 402C – also played its part when, on the afternoon after Bishop's murder, Lieutenant Commander Tomlin and Major Robin Keaney, recently retired from the Royal Air Force, conducted an aerial survey of Grenada where they noted little by way of military activity save for the arrival of an An-26 transport at Pearls airfield and that the runway at Salines was blocked, with all construction work on the new airport being stopped. They noted no deployment of anti-aircraft batteries and were not challenged during their flight.[18]

While the BDF Air Wing was playing its small part, Commander Roger Porteous, a Royal Navy officer on secondment to the Barbados Coast Guard and the Regional Security System, was compiling a comprehensive report on all the beaches and bays along Grenada's coastline with a view to identifying potential areas suitable for amphibious landings. He recommended the Grand Anse and Grand Mal bays on the west coast of Grenada.[19] This was to prove invaluable to the planning of the 22nd Marine Amphibious Unit which was to eventually land troops and armour at Grand Mal on 25 October 1983. The lack of knowledge of Grenada, its coast and its geography was to become one of the major issues that plagued the planning of Operation Urgent Fury.

The RSS and the BDF also provided critical intelligence to the United States with the CIA representative in Barbados posing some 18 questions to the two agencies. The shocking realisation that the CIA had no inkling of who among the People's Revolutionary Government still remained loyal to Bishop, who was effectively in command of the PRA, or who within the cabinet was actively supporting Bernard Coard. Worst of all, US intelligence had no accurate knowledge as to the location of the several hundred American students attending university at Grenada based campuses. In these areas, the RSS and the BDF provided much needed assistance.[20]

When the Caribbean Peacekeeping Force was established, Colonel Rudyard Lewis was promoted to Brigadier General and given the role of regional coordinator, as well as being the Chief of Staff of the BDF. Actual command of the CPKF was placed in the more able and experienced hands of Colonel Ken Barnes of the Jamaica Defence Force, which contributed the single largest contingent of troops to the CPKF and were the only ones regarded as being combat capable by the Americans.[21] The BDF contributed a reinforced rifle platoon of 50 combat personnel while over 100 personnel of the RBPF, armed with an eclectic mix of 7.62mm SLRs and 0.303 Rifle No.4 Mk.1s, spearheaded a force of police personnel from OECS states. These police forces were instrumental in rebuilding the shattered Royal Grenada Police Force and in maintaining law and order on the island.

As can be seen, the BDF played an important role in the early stages of planning the intervention in Grenada, far outweighing its small actual military participation in the CPKF. The BDF staff officers, acting in concert with the RSS, were able to utilise its limited physical and human resources to provide invaluable intelligence about Grenada and the disposition of PRA troops and, more importantly, their state of apparent readiness. The plan for a rescue operation to free Prime Minister Bishop might, had it been executed promptly, have worked had the plan been taken more seriously but that should not detract from the excellent performance of the BDF.

The Barbados Defence Force Today

The BDF is a small service with under 1,000 active and reserve personnel. It has no Air Wing but its land forces and coast guard fulfil their respective army and naval roles.

Land Forces

The primary role of the Barbados Defence Force (BDF) is the defence of Barbados against external aggression, although in practice the force focuses on counter-narcotics operations and support to the Royal Barbados Police Force. The BDF also participates in Humanitarian Assistance and Disaster Relief (HADR) operations within its limited resources. The BDF's land force element is the Barbados Regiment, which is comprised of one regular battalion and one reserve battalion. The regiment's primary combat element is a single Special Operations Company that is trained for special operations, marine support, and light infantry roles. Equipment is confined to infantry personal weapons of American and British origin.[24] The Barbados Regiment has no heavy support weapons or armoured vehicles and even lacks mortars for fire support. This means that, unlike Jamaica, which has been able to deploy a full rifle company, supported with a medical section and a mortar section for deployment overseas, as was the case with Urgent Fury in 1983, the BDF is limited to deploying platoon sized units and these without support weapons.

The current organisational framework marks a shift from the early days of the Barbados Regiment which had initially tried to model itself on a small infantry battalion, organised and equipped conventionally. The emphasis on a Special Operations Company, aided by the Technical Support Company for engineering and mechanical support, the whole being administered by the Headquarters Company, has turned the land force element into a more flexible entity with an emphasis on a small, highly-trained combat element which is able to provide a quick-reaction force to cater for the country's security as well as to provide a deployable element for external peacekeeping operations. The latter are rare but

Table 7: The BDF today

	Total Strength	Army	Air Force	Navy
Active personnel	630 est. [22]	430 est.	0	200
Reserves	300 est. [23]	250 est.	0	50 est.

as has been seen, Barbados has a penchant for taking a leadership role in such ventures.

The BDF land forces also have a useful reserve in the form of a three-company element plus a coast guard reserve. The former includes a headquarters company plus two rifle companies. This means, that with reserve mobilisation, Barbados can field a battalion sized combat element though one which lacks support weapons. It should be noted that the Barbados Regiment reserve still uses older pattern rifles and machine guns and is still awaiting the new M16 rifles that now dominate the regiment's inventory and which are also increasingly used by the RBPF. It is of further interest that the reserve element of the BDF is responsible for the regiment's colours and upholding its traditions, leaving the regular force to concentrate on honing its skills as a Special Operations Company. The unit participates in joint exercises with foreign countries and is quite proficient though lacking in specialised surveillance equipment and support weapons.

The BDF's land elements, while sufficient for limited internal security operations, lack the strength to defend the country against external attack. However, given the limited threats facing Barbados, the force is sufficient to meet most challenges. At present, the land forces are playing an increasing role in supporting the police with the task of patrolling the coastline to prevent smuggling and other illicit activities.

The BDF land forces have been increasingly employed, since the 1990s, on operations with the RBPF, the latter still largely operating as a civilian constabulary and has not emulated the trend towards intense militarisation that has been seen in Trinidad and Tobago and Jamaica. In the latter two countries, police armament and uniforms have been radically altered to give the respective forces a quasi-military look.

Barbados, despite a more widespread issue of firearms to its constabulary, has not gone down this path. Therefore, in joint BDF-RBPF operations, the roles and responsibilities of the respective personnel is well defined and the differences in approach, orientation and equipment has worked well together. While police unions have criticised the BDF for getting involved with policing tasks, they have produced good results.[25]

The BDF Coast Guard

From the 1990s onwards, the Barbados Defence Force (BDF) Coast Guard's core tasks are counter-narcotics operations and surveillance and policing of the country's Exclusive Economic Zone. The old fleet of ships, led by the ageing *Trident*, was increasingly unable to secure the country's interests in its maritime domain. In the 1990s, the BDF Coast Guard's capability declined in relative terms just as the threat from narcotics trafficking and associated trans-national organised crime began to increase at a significant pace.

In order to carry out these missions, the coast guard needs to be substantially expanded and modernised. While personnel strength has registered a modest increase, to some 200 personnel, the fleet has been completely recapitalised.

It is hard to overstate the importance of the steps the BDF Coast Guard took to recapitalise itself. By the 1990s, it was increasingly clear the that the old *Trident* was past its prime. Set against this was the increasing employment by smugglers of faster vessels and that the vessels acquired to supplement the *Trident* were hopelessly outclassed.

The modernisation got underway in 2007 when the Coast Guard inducted into service three modern Damen Stan Patrol 4207 offshore patrol vessels and two shorter-range high-speed Stan Patrol 1204 patrol craft. This has allowed the retirement of older vessels, with the *Trident* being one of the last to be decommissioned and scuttled, largely for sentimental reasons – with the name passing to the first of the new SPa 4207s. The Damen vessels were selected to provide a cost-effective patrol solution for the BDF Coast Guard's maritime requirement and were the second such sale in the Caribbean – Jamaica being the first in 2005.

The SPa 4207s are armed with 0.50-inch M2HB machine guns and while they have radar, do not have any FLIR systems, thus limiting their surveillance capabilities at night. Serviceability of the SPa 4207s has been respectable but deployment was temporarily restricted during 2010–2015 due to financial difficulties leading to crew restrictions and fuel shortages.

The Barbados Coast Guard is sufficiently equipped to perform its primary duties of patrolling and policing Barbados's territorial waters and engaging in counter-narcotics operations. It is not prepared to undertake conventional operations. Of note, Barbados recently developed an Integrated Coastal Surveillance System to assist with anti-drug trafficking operations.[26]

The Barbados Coast Guard works with the Regional Security System for the purposes of enhancing Caribbean collective security. In particular, the RSS's two C-26A aircraft provide the BDF Coast Guard with a proxy maritime surveillance capability. The aircraft are equipped with radar and FLIR systems but are unarmed and have very limited transport capability, severely limiting their flexibility.

The Barbados Coast Guard participates in exercise Tradewinds, which is organised by US SOUTHCOM and which is a necessary tool to promote regional cooperation and provide training to Caribbean security forces to address drug trafficking, organised crime, human and weapons trafficking, and illegal fishing. Marijuana seizures doubled between 2014 and 2015, largely as a result of more effective patrolling by the Barbados Coast Guard.[27]

The coast guard is building an Integrated Coastal Surveillance System (ICSS). Design of the systems began in 2009 and the system became operational in 2014.[28] The network consists of four fixed 360-degree coverage radar stations, which are supposed to be capable of covering the entire territory of Barbados.

Based around the Elta M-2226 radar, the project includes a National Command and Control Center (NCCC), radars, E/O cameras, Automatic Identification System (AIS), meteorological sensors and other supporting infrastructure. The entire

Table 8: BDF Surface Fleet

Class	Manufacturer	Role	Original Total	In Service	Commissioned
Stan Patrol 4207	Damen Shipyards	Offshore patrol craft	3	3	2007
Stan Patrol 1204	Damen Shipyards	Inshore patrol craft	2	2	2008
Dauntless	SeaArk Marine, Monticello	Inshore patrol craft	2	1	1999
Zodiac 920	Zodiac	Rigid inflatable boat	1	1	2004
Zodiac 921	Zodiac	Rigid inflatable boat	1	1	2004
RIB 1000	Damen Shipyards	Rigid inflatable boat	3	3	2007

A Damen SPa 4207-class HMBS *Rudyard Lewis* of the Barbados Defence Force. (Damen Shipyards)

arrangement is very similar to one in use in Trinidad and, like its Trinidadian counterpart, is also undergoing an upgrade.[29]

Conclusion

The Barbados Defence Force is the smallest of the forces being discussed in this book yet the country has a rich and varied military history with participation in several operations – though not taking part in combat – outside of its territory. The BDF's land forces, though small, are optimised to meet the likely security threats facing the island while its Coast Guard is a reasonably well-equipped force capable of exercising control over the country's maritime domain. However, the country lacks any of its own air assets, compromising the effectiveness of the BDF.

4

GUYANA

Guyana, or more officially the Co-operative Republic of Guyana, is a country on the northern mainland of South America. Its capital city is Georgetown and the country is bordered by the Atlantic Ocean to the north, Brazil to the south and southwest, Venezuela to the west, and Suriname to the east. Its land area encompasses some 215,000 square kilometres (83,000 square miles), making it the third-smallest sovereign state by area in mainland South America after Uruguay and Suriname. However, of all the countries under discussion in this book, it is by far the largest, though, with a population of only about 750,000 people,[1] it has a significantly smaller population than Trinidad and Tobago and only about a quarter of the population of Jamaica.

Politics and Demographics

The demographics of the country, which are closely tied to its politics, are largely a mix of descendants of Indian indentured labourers and African slaves. The largest ethnic group are the Indo-Guyanese at 39.8 percent of the population, according to the 2012 census. They are followed by the Afro-Guyanese, at 29.3 percent. A sizeable population of Guyanese of mixed heritage make up 19.9 percent of the population. Unlike the islands of the Caribbean, where they are virtually non-existent as distinct groups, indigenous peoples (known locally as Amerindians) make up 10.5 percent of the population.[2]

Guyana's political history, closely linked to race and, in the past, very violent, is dominated by two main political parties – the Indo-Guyanese dominated People's Progressive Party (PPP) and the Afro-Guyanese dominated People's National Congress (PNC). The antagonism between these two parties has been the tragedy of Guyana and the armed forces have been compromised by their past affiliation to the former.

Prior to independence from the United Kingdom, a transitional government existed until elections in 1957 led to a reconstituted Legislative Council with 14 elected members. The PPP won all but two seats, but split into two factions, one led by Dr Cheddi Jagan and the other by Forbes Burnham, who would soon become implacable political enemies. After a round of constitutional reform in 1961 elections were again won by the PPP, which secured 20 of the 35 directly-elected seats. However, the PPP had only received 1.6 percent more of the vote than the new People's National Congress (PNC), led by Burnham but had won almost double the number of seats thanks to the first past the post system. Violent mass demonstrations led by the PNC, a general strike and severe inter-racial violence followed, with reports of the CIA being involved in an effort to oust the socialist Cheddi Jagan. After a few weeks the British authorities intervened by sending in troops and the Governor declared a state of emergency which was aimed at neutralising Jagan in favour of Burnham.[3]

The British authorities then engineered a series of further constitutional reforms which created a unicameral 54-member House of Assembly elected by proportional representation. The first elections held under the new system took place in 1964. The PPP again emerged as the largest party but the PNC was able to form a coalition government with the United Force. Jagan, sensing foul play by the British, refused to resign and had to be removed by Governor Richard Luyt, with Burnham replacing him, to commence a 28-year de facto dictatorship.

Following Guyana's independence in 1966, the House of Assembly was renamed the National Assembly but all subsequent elections, until 1992, were rigged by the PNC. The rigged elections continued in 1968 and 1973 and no respite was found when a new constitution was promulgated in 1980. This led to the creation of an executive president; the leader of the party that received the most votes in an election would automatically assume the post, which naturally meant, after the rigged 1980 elections, that Forbes Burnham would be president. The elections of 1985 were also rigged but Burnham's death in 1985 saw him succeeded by Desmond Hoyte who faced the economic catastrophe wrought by Burnham's flawed economic policies.

Hoyte was no paragon of democratic virtue but the end of the Cold War led to demands from Western countries and international organisations for democratic reforms which were introduced in the late 1980s. After many delays, free and fair elections were held in 1992. The result was a victory for the PPP, with Cheddi Jagan returning to power after a 28-year gap.[4]

The PPP went on to win the next elections in 1997 though Hoyte sought to challenge the results with an overt appeal to the Afro-Guyanese dominated security forces to support their 'kith and kin'. Under sustained but unfair pressure, the PPP agreed to early elections and in 2001 the electoral system was modified. Elections later that year saw another PPP victory, replicated in 2006.

The elections held in 2011 saw the PPP win the largest number of seats (32), but fail to achieve a majority. Thanks to the Burnham era rule where the head of the largest party would become president, the then PPP leader Donald Ramotar became president.

In 2015, tired of electoral losses, all of the parliamentary opposition parties (the Alliance for Change and the four-member Alliance for Progress and National Unity (APNU), which included the PNC) formed a single electoral front. This alliance won 33 seats, allowing PNC leader David A. Granger to become president. However, it fell in a vote of no-confidence in December 2018 and after some bizarre and frankly nonsensical court challenges, fresh elections were finally held on 2 March 2020.

Those elections were eventually won by the PPP, allowing Dr Irfaan Ali to assume office as the country's president. The 2020 General Elections, saw the most overt and brazen attempt at electoral fraud, perpetrated by loyalists of the incumbent government (the PNC and its allied parties) and this was only thwarted by determined legal action on the part of the PPP and the intervention of CARICOM, the United States, Great Britain and Canada who stood firm in their commitment to a transparent counting of votes. The PNC and its allies subverted elements in the Guyana Election Commission and the matter ended up in the courts with some judges showing a blatant level of favouritism to the PNC. Ultimately, the Caribbean Court of Justice, Guyana's final appellate court, ruled decisively against the rigging attempts, followed by a Guyana Court of Appeal decision to block a brazen attempt by PNC elements to disqualify tens of thousands of votes on spurious grounds. Dr Irfaan Ali assumed office on 2 August 2020, some five months after the elections were held.[5]

Economy

Guyana, with a newly discovered bounty of crude oil reserves, has the fastest growing economy in the world with a projected GDP growth of 26.2 percent in 2020. This very high growth masks the fact that Guyana is starting from an astonishingly low level, especially considering the country's bountiful natural and mineral reserves. Over the last decade, Guyana had an economic growth rate of 4.2 percent per annum but even now, some 35 percent of the population lives below the poverty line. Guyana's economy is dominated by agriculture and mining. Sugar, bauxite, rice, and gold account for between 70 and 75 percent of export earnings, though this will soon change as oil revenues begin to dominate the economy. Of concern to Guyana is the relatively low skill level of much of its workforce, thus making it dependent on personnel from overseas for the oil industry.

International Disputes and National Security

Of all the countries of the English-speaking Caribbean, Guyana is unique in respect of the depth of the military threat it faces from a much more powerful adversary – Venezuela. Esequibo (or Essequibo), is a disputed territory of 159,500 square kilometres in area, located to the west of the Essequibo River. It is administered and controlled by Guyana but claimed by Venezuela. The dispute is one inherited from the countries' respective colonial pasts with disputes between Spain (in the case of Venezuela) and the Netherlands and the United Kingdom (in the case of Guyana).[6]

The legal status of the region is subject to the Geneva Agreement, which was signed by the United Kingdom, Venezuela and British Guiana on 17 February 1966 – just prior to Guyana's independence. This treaty mandates that the parties will agree to find a practical, peaceful and satisfactory solution to the dispute. In 1970, the Port of Spain Protocol was signed to give some formality to the need for a peaceful resolution.[7]

However, because Essequibo is an oil-rich area that borders both countries and is estimated to have between 800 million and 1.4 billion barrels of high quality crude oil, worth at least US$ 44 billion, the intensity of interest in the region has risen to the fore in recent years, with both the Venezuelan government and opposition being entirely in accord in supporting Venezuela's claim to the region. It should be noted that this area is so large, it effectively means that Venezuela claims 40 percent of Guyana's territory.

For decades the issue was largely dormant, but the dispute over Essequibo once again took prominence in January 2013 when Venezuela intercepted and detained an oil exploration vessel working on behalf of the Guyanese government.[8] At this time, US energy companies Exxon Mobil and Hess discovered huge oil reserves in the territory.[9] Exxon Mobil later moved with alacrity with plans to exploit the Stabroek Block. This has led to renewed tension between Guyana and Venezuela. Exxon Mobil has allied itself with the Guyanese government and supports its claims against Venezuela. This might be in part due to the fact that Venezuela nationalised US$ 10 billion of the company's assets some ten years ago. This, as might be expected, did not go down well with the company but also means that Guyana is now effectively supported by a powerful multinational corporation with the ear of the United States government.

In 2015, Venezuela's president Nicolas Maduro signed a decree soon after the announcement of the oil discovery, that established what was termed a 'defence' zone offshore that would, if this zone were to be enforced, give Guyana no direct access to the Atlantic Ocean. As per Venezuela's Official Gazette of 27 May 2015, President Nicolas Maduro effectively authorised Venezuela's sovereignty over the coastal waters west of the Essequibo River to Delta Amacuro. This would mean that Venezuela now claims all the waters off Essequibo, including the area where Exxon Mobil is seeking to exploit Guyana's oil reserves.[10]

There has been little evidence to suggest that Venezuela has moved aggressively to do any such rigorous enforcement, beyond harassing and detaining oil exploration vessels. One of the most brazen incidents being on 23 December 2018 when a Venezuelan naval vessel and its helicopter intercepted a seismic survey ship doing work for Exxon Mobil.[11]

Tension between the two countries has led the US Coast Guard to join their Guyanese counterparts in joint exercises and patrols while Guyana has moved some of its meagre forces to provide a veneer of border security while Venezuelan Su-30MKVs violate its airspace with impunity.[12]

Guyana's smaller neighbour, Suriname also claims the territory east of Guyana's New River. This is a largely uninhabited area of some 15,000 square kilometres in southeast Guyana and there have been periodic tensions over this region but no fighting since 1966. However, Guyana and Suriname, at one time, also had differences over their offshore maritime boundaries. This dispute, dormant for decades, came to the fore in June 2000 when a Canadian company came to drill for oil under a Guyanese concession. The dispute with Suriname was arbitrated by the United Nations Tribunal on the Law of the Sea and a ruling in favour of Guyana was given in September 2007, thus bringing an end to this dispute.[13]

Both countries elected new governments and presidents in 2020 and both Dr Irfaan Ali of Guyana and Chan Santhoki of Suriname have moved to promote cooperation between their countries.

The GDF Evolution – 1964 to 1992

The Guyana Defence Force (GDF) has its roots in the British Guyana Volunteer Force (BGVF) which was formed in June 1948.[14] This followed in the tradition of a long line of volunteer militias used by the British in their Caribbean colonies. The force succeeded the British Guyana Militia, formed in 1891, and which served into the Second World War. The BGVF was ostensibly under the Commissioner of Police, though the force had its own commanding officer. This dual control persisted until 1957 when it was replaced by a single line of command with the BGVF finally having its own commanding officer.

GDF personnel with a Chinese-made Type-63 multiple rocket launcher. (GDF)

GDF ambulance with a GDF Air Wing Bell 206 helicopter. (GDF)

The BGVF was structured like a then typical British territorial infantry battalion with an authorised maximum strength of 600 officers and men. By 1963, manpower was organised into a battalion headquarters, a headquarters company and five rifle companies. The battalion headquarters and 'A' and 'C' companies were located at Eve Leary, Georgetown, and 'B' company, in New Amsterdam, Berbice. 'D' company was formed in Mackenzie in the Upper Demerara River in 1957 and 'E' company was formed on the West Coast Demerara in 1963. The force was largely part-time with a small full-time establishment. It was armed with standard British infantry weapons – .303 No.4 Mk 1 Enfield rifles; .303 Mk 1 Vickers machine guns; .303 Bren light machine guns; .380 revolvers; and 9mm Sten submachine guns.[15]

The BGVF served as the country's primary military force until the 1960s when a police Special Service Unit, under Major Raymond Sattaur was formed to allay concerns about the impartiality of the Afro-Guyanese dominated BGVF during racial riots. The BGVF and the SSU were to eventually evolve into the Guyana Defence Force which came into being in 1966, the BGVF being dissolved as a consequence of the new military's formation.[16]

Unfortunately, the racial politics of Guyana were to be infectious and, as will be seen, the new GDF would find itself heavily involved in the political arena as a willing agent of the Burnham regime and was deemed to be a heavily politicised organisation.

The Guyana Defence Force – Ground Forces

The Guyana Defence Force as initially established in 1966, had a single infantry battalion with three rifle companies. Their .303 Enfield rifles were replaced by 7.62mm L1A1 SLRs and NATO standard machine guns in 1967. These three rifle companies were joined in 1967 by a specialised Reconnaissance Platoon which had some of the GDF's best troops and had six Land Rover utility vehicles, one 3-tonne truck and, more importantly, four Shorland armoured cars.[17] This formation was the cutting edge of the fledgling GDF and the four Shorlands were the only armoured vehicles to serve the GDF, despite later rumours of EE-11 Urutus being delivered in the 1980s.

The GDF land force element was to grow exponentially in size in the 1970s and 1980s with multiple battalions being added with some two infantry and one Guard Battalion, one artillery battalion, one special forces battalion, an engineering battalion and a service support battalion being on strength at the peak of the GDF. The 11th and 12th infantry battalions were formed in 1975 with the 13th Guard Battalion being formed in 1976.[18] This meant that the GDF was a brigade-sized formation with strong combat arm with support weapons, supported by an adequate logistics and transport infrastructure.

The biggest development in the GDF was the spectacular growth of its artillery component. The mortar platoon came into existence in November 1967 with the purchase of nine 81mm Israeli Soltam mortars and with a personnel strength of one officer and 31 other ranks. Additional 82mm and 120mm mortars were acquired from the communist bloc as Guyana's government turned to Cuba, China, the Democratic People's Republic of Korea (DPRK) and the Soviet Union for arms and support.[19]

The mortar platoon became the Support Weapons Command in August 1976 when 61 soldiers of the GDF completed training in Cuba on three classes of artillery weapons – mortars, tube artillery and anti-aircraft guns. The Support Weapons Command now comprised an HQ Group, A Group (122mm artillery), B Group

GDF troops with aquad-barrel 14.5mm ZPU-4 machine gun. (GDF)

A GDF soldier with an old Kalashnikov AK-47/AKM assault rifle during an exercise. (GDF)

(81mm, 82mm, 120mm mortars), and C Group (7.62mm FN MAG, 12.7mm and 14.5mm anti-aircraft machine guns). More soldiers of the Support Weapons Command were sent to the DPRK for further training in 1978 on 76mm ZiS-3 artillery and the 14.5mm ZPU-4 anti-aircraft guns. A year later, the unit was renamed the Support Weapons Battalion.[20]

In 1980, twelve 122mm artillery pieces arrived from the DPRK and in 1983 the first shipment of 76mm ZiS-3 artillery, 107mm rocket launchers, aquatic, anti-personnel and anti-tank mines, grenades and ammunition for the 76mm cannon and 107mm rocket launcher arrived at Linden. Training of 17 officers and 194 other ranks on the employment of the 76mm guns, 107mm rocket launcher, and the 82mm and 120mm mortars was carried out in 1984, by which time the unit was renamed the 1st Artillery Battalion.[21]

The GDF Infantry Brigade was redesignated the Ground Forces Group (GFG) and, as such, 12 Company of the Artillery Battalion, operating 82mm and 120mm mortars, was transferred to the GFG as the 141 Support Company in 1984. With the mortars now with the new unit, 12 Company, reinforced with 65 newly trained troops, became responsible for the 76mm ZiS-3 guns.[22]

In 1986, with Desmond Hoyte's government, began a gradual reduction in strength of the GDF, with the 13 Guard Battalion being disbanded that year. However, the artillery battalion continued training with new 82mm recoilless rifles being produced, and maintenance and advanced training being conducted on the other weapons in the inventory. In March 1987, 112 Company and 12 Company merged to form one company operating the 76mm and 122mm cannons as manpower reductions continued.[23]

The GDF GFG began to be reduced further in strength with the four surviving infantry battalions being reduced to two and then to one. By 1992, when free and fair elections were held after a gap of 28 years, the Ground Forces Group was reduced to the 1st Infantry Battalion Group as the principal combat unit with the 2nd Infantry Battalion Group being formed with a combination of regular soldiers and part-time reservists/militia. By this time, the artillery battalion was reduced in strength and is known now as the 21st Artillery Company with mortars and 76mm guns.

The Guyana Defence Force Air Corps

The Air Wing of the GDF was created in 1968 as the Guyana Defence Force Air Wing. In 1970 it was renamed the Air Command, GDF and three years later, renamed again as the Guyana Defence Force Air Corps.[24] The Air Corps, as it remains, has its headquarters at Camp Ayanganna in Georgetown. Its main operational base is Georgetown's Cheddi Jagan Airport, with its small fleet of transport aircraft and helicopters making extensive use of the nation's network of small, underdeveloped airstrips. At present, the primary missions of the Air Corps are transportation, communications, and liaison. It has been assigned the secondary missions including counter-narcotics and maritime patrolling but has never developed the assets to do either.

The GDF Air Wing began with a small force of three Helio H-295 Super Couriers delivered in 1968 to form the main operational assets of the Air Wing. These aircraft were used extensively on reconnaissance operations during the two rather vicious, albeit short, conflicts in the Rupununi region and in the New River area in 1969 and were useful liaison assets for the new, and still small GDF.[25] However, their very limited payload meant that for transport operations, the larger aircraft of Guyana Airways were used – to great effect in both of the 1969 conflicts.

A significant expansion of the Air Wing began in the early 1970s when the first of seven BN-2 Islanders were delivered. These aircraft proved very popular in Guyanese service and a number continue in use to date with two acquired second-hand in 2018. The first helicopters were delivered in 1975, with a couple of Alouette III followed by a number of Bell 206B and Bell 212 helicopters, delivery of which began in 1976. The Bell 206B remains in service while the Alouette IIIs and the Bell 212s were withdrawn from use in 1982 and 1994 respectively.

Fixed wing transport assets were never large in number and a single example of the Beech Super King Air 200 was joined by a single Cessna 206 Stationair in 1975. Four years later, the first of four Shorts Skyvan aircraft arrived and even today the type remains in use – albeit, like the Islanders, in the form of recently purchased second-hand airframes. A Cessna 182 Skylane and an Embraer EMB-110 were acquired in the 1980s but neither lasted long in service. A solitary Y-12 from China was delivered in 2002 and remains in limited service although there are signs of extensive corrosion on the aircraft leading to questions over its continuation in service without major repairs.

A flirtation with the USSR led to the delivery of three Mi-8 helicopters in 1985 but these were reduced to derelicts within a few years of service and their abandoned airframes are still to be seen.

Shorts Skyvans of the GDF Air Wing. (DPI)

Table 9: Aircraft operated by the GDF Air Wing/Air Command/Air Corps over the last four decades[26]

Aircraft Type	Quantity	Service Entry	Out of Service	Origin
Aerospatiale SA 319B Alouette III	2	1975	1982	France
Beech Super King Air 200	1	1975	1992	USA
Bell 206B JetRanger	4	1976	current	USA
Bell 212	3	1976	1994	USA
Bell 412SP	1	1984	current	USA
Britten-Norman BN-2A Islander	7	1971	1998	UK
Cessna 182J Skylane	1	1982	1994	USA
Cessna 206 Stationair	1	1975	1995	USA
Embraer EMB-110P Bandeirante	1	1984	1994	Brazil
Harbin Y-12 Panda	1	2002	current	China
Helio H-295 Super Courier	3	1968	1971	USA
Mil Mi-8 Hip	3	1985	1991	Russia
Rotorway 162F	2	2004	current	USA
Short SC.7 Skyvan 3M	5	1979	current	UK

A better fate awaited Bell 412 helicopters, of which a single example remains in service.

The Guyana Defence Force Coast Guard

On 9 January 1967 the maritime arm of the Guyana Defence Force was established. This unit had an initial strength of one officer and 22 other ranks. SPO St Lewis, the longest serving member of the Coast Guard, was amongst the 22 other ranks.[27]

The first vessels for the force were built at the Sprostons dockyard. These were four steel hulled vessels – *Camoudi*, *Labaria*, *Rattler* and *Hymeraly* and they were built with caterpillar engines and were designed to transport Land Rovers and 32 troops each, dramatically enhancing the transport capabilities of the GDF but added nothing by way of patrol assets to the Maritime Command.[28]

Riverine patrol assets were boosted when three 40ft river patrol launches from England – the *Jaguar*, *Ocelot* and *Morgay* – were received in 1969. These were very short-lived – *Morgay* was destroyed by fire, while *Ocelot* and *Jaguar* were decommissioned a few years later. Needing to boost patrol assets, in 1975 the trawler *Ekereku* was acquired and converted into an interim patrol vessel.[29]

The biggest boost was received in 1976 when the maritime command acquired a coastal patrol craft from England. The new vessel, the Peccari DFS 1010, a 103ft patrol craft, arrived in Georgetown in 1977, making the transatlantic voyage from the United Kingdom under its own power. The vessel was powered by two Paxmon high-speed engines, was fully air-conditioned, her main source of electricity was two petbow generators, and she was armed with two 20mm guns, one forward and one aft, plus several machine guns. The ship had a crew of seven officers and 22 ratings who were involved with the project from construction to completion and who sailed the vessel from the UK to Guyana, thus making the first and only time that the GDF undertook this operation.[30]

In GDF Maritime Command service, the Peccari conducted mainly fisheries protection patrols and served for some ten years, making a large number of seizures of Korean trawlers. The vessel had a sprint speed of 27kts, cruised at 15kts and had an endurance of two weeks, with patrols being evolved around that limitation.[31]

Unfortunately, the vessel had some inherent problems. The deck of the vessel was made of marine plywood which was, rather surprisingly, difficult to obtain in Guyana and weakened over time. As is unfortunately common in the Caribbean, there was a shortage of funding for the maintenance of the vessel. As such, after only ten years of service, the Peccari was effectively unserviceable by 1986 and the derelict hulk remained at anchor for five years before finally being decommissioned in 1991, leaving the GDF without any major seagoing assets.

Once again, the communist bloc was approached for assistance and in 1979 two fast attack craft (FAC) were acquired from the Democratic People's Republic of Korea, the DF 1011 and 1012 – believed to be based on the Sin Hung torpedo boat – and armed with 14.5mm KPV machine guns. These vessels did not last long in service and were withdrawn from use after only a few years in commission.[32]

Six additional vessels were acquired from the German Democratic Republic. Three of these were Inshore Patrol vessels (IPV) known as SABs – *Hassar* (AFIVIS), *Houri* (DFIOIA) and Pirai (DF10200). The other three were riverine patrol vessels, known as the Grasshoppers – DF1013, DF1014 and DF1015. None of these assets were ocean-going assets but did aid the GDF in maintaining a robust riverine presence.[33]

To boost ocean-going assets, the *Makandra II*, a fishing trawler seized during operations, was given to the maritime command, she was later renamed *Maipuri* (DF 1017) and converted to a patrol vessel. Some use was made of other seized trawlers but these were of very limited utility and, at one time, the force had to make use of two shrimp boats. Amphibious assets were augmented by a single landing craft of the Kimbala-class, produced by the Damen Shipyard group.

These modest assets were the sole vessels available to the GDF over the decades of its existence, with riverine forces receiving some attention with locally built launches and boats operating in support of the GDF's ground forces. A number of floating river bases were established to enhance the efficacy of the river patrols.

However, by the 1990s, it was abundantly clear that the GDF maritime forces were wholly inadequate to protect the country's maritime interests and with the loss of the Peccari, the force had no ability to operate in the country's Exclusive Economic Zone and lacked any appreciable combat capability. During the late 1990s, the government of the then President Bharrat Jagdeo made some efforts to recapitalise the GDF and the maritime command – renamed the Coast Guard. To this end, a rather controversial purchase of the ex-Royal Navy River-class minesweeper, HMS *Orwell*, was made and the vessel entered service in 2001. Its 40mm guns were replaced by 20mm Hispano-Suiza weapons and this vessel remains the sole ocean-going vessel of the GDF. However, this vessel was never particularly effective in its assigned role and numerous operational issues reduced its operation efficacy and the vessel remains largely inoperable. Four US Motor Life Boats of the T-44-class were also delivered in 2001.[34]

Metal Shark patrol vessels of the GDF Coast Guard. (GDF)

GDFS *Essequibo*: Flagship of the GDF Coast Guard. (DPI)

A trio of Metal Shark riverine patrol boats of the GDF Coast Guard. (GDF)

The Rupununi Uprising 1969

Three weeks after Guyana's blatantly rigged elections of December 1968, large ranch owners, supported by their Amerindian employees, sought to secede from Guyana and sought to establish a government of the 'Republic of Rupununi', in the southernmost and most remote part of Guyana, in January 1969. The movement was led by the 27-year-old Valerie Hart, a United Front candidate in the rigged elections of 1968 and who participated in the First Conference of Amerindian Leaders, named the 'Cabacaburi Congress', in 1968. This conference, concerned with the Afro-centric and discriminatory policies of Forbes Burnham, sought to present the concerns of the 40,000 Amerindian residents of the region.[35]

However, these concerns were not particularly well received by the Burnham administration which seemed somewhat oblivious to the extent of the potential difficulties that Guyana could face and the risk of a violent uprising in the region. Indeed, Guyanese Agriculture Minister, Robert Jordan, went so far as to declare that the government would not recognise the inhabitants' land ownership certifications and indicated that the lands would be given to members of the Afro-Guyanese population of Guyana.[36] Following this insensitivity, Valerie Hart was appointed as the President of the Provisional Government Committee of Rupununi.

Of particular importance, especially given the remoteness of the region, was the nexus between the insurrectionists and Venezuela. There is little doubt of a nexus since Valerie Hart openly stated that she would support Venezuela taking control of the disputed Essequibo region and, with this in mind, a number of ranchers and their supporters went to Venezuela to receive arms and training. The forces available to the insurrectionists were not large but, given the size of the area and the paucity of Guyanese police personnel in the region, they believed

Combat Experience – 1969

The GDF had a rather dramatic introduction to combat only three years after its formation. Prior to 1969, the GDF had been principally seen as an internal security force supporting the Guyana Police Force (GPF). This would change rather dramatically in 1969 when its nascent combat capability proved to be invaluable.

that their forces would suffice to achieve their ill-defined political objectives.

The rebels launched a vicious attack on the town of Lethem on 2 January 1969. Fifty years later, writing in Guyana's *Stabroek News* newspaper, former GDF Chief of Staff (and later president) David Granger was to recall the attack as follows:

> On arriving at Lethem, the rebels opened fire on the police station with the man-portable M-9 Anti-Tank rocket launcher (the so-called bazooka) and automatic weapons. Policemen rushing out of the building were shot dead. The rebels then entered the station and shot and killed one civilian employee, Victor Hernandez. The police inspector who was at the District Commissioner's office at the time of the attack was shot and killed there.
>
> The government dispenser who rushed to the police station when the firing began was shot at and wounded. The station's radio communication with police headquarters in Georgetown ceased immediately after the attack began and before any messages about it could be sent. In all, six persons were killed at Lethem. The rebels then rounded up the residents including the District Commissioner and held them prisoner in the abattoir, blocked the airstrip and set up machine gun posts at tactical positions around the township.
>
> Elsewhere in the district, other sections of the rebel force were despatched to block the airstrips at Good Hope, Karasabai, Karanambo and Annai; seize the small police stations at Annai and Good Hope; and shut down radio communications. This left open only the airstrip at Manari about 9 km (6 miles) from Lethem.
>
> Apart from the mayhem in Lethem, the rebel offensive had the effect of forcing hundreds of Amerindians to flee. About 300 crossed the Takutu River at St Ignatius to seek refuge in Bom Fin, Brazil. Others fled to the hills or hid in the bush. About 95 fugitives, probably members of the Melville-Hart clan, initially arrived at Santa Elena where they were granted asylum and promised land and employment by the Venezuelan government.[37]

Despite this violence, the rebels were doomed to fail. The Guyana Defence Force responded with three rifle companies from Lieutenant Colonel Cecil Martindale's 2nd Infantry Battalion. These were No. 2 Company under Captain Vernon Williams; No. 4 Company under Captain Desmond Roberts; and No. 6 Company under Lieutenant Joseph Singh.

These troops arrived at the Manari airstrip and quickly re-established control, arresting 30 rebels and causing the leaders to flee to Venezuela. They also recovered the bodies of slain police personnel, police officers Inspector Whittington Braithwaite, Sergeant Benedict Sukra, Constables James McKenzie, William Norton, and Kendall Michael, and civilian Victor Hernandez. Thus ended the somewhat grandiose dreams of the rebels and while there may have been some reprisal violence, it does not appear to have been widespread.

Operation Climax 1969 – Suriname and Guyana Clash

Guyana and Suriname had a significant, although bloodless, military clash in 1969 in the New River area where the two countries have an ongoing border dispute. Like so many of the tensions between post-colonial nations, this dispute is an old one between Guyana's British colonial master and Suriname's Dutch rulers. However, in 1969, while Guyana had been independent for three years, Suriname was still a Dutch colony and its military forces were the 1,100 strong Troepenmacht in Suriname (TRIS) which was recruited locally and had responsibility for the security of Suriname but remained under Dutch command. This force scrupulously avoided confrontations with Guyanese troops and ensured that no misunderstandings and unnecessary tensions emerged.[38]

However, in 1967, Premier Johan Adolf Pengel, whose political credibility had taken several severe blows, and with tensions increasing between his own Creole-dominated National Party of Suriname (NPS) and the Indo-Surinamese (Hindustani) dominated United Hindustani Party (VHP) political parties, began to escalate the rhetorical war between Guyana and Suriname with a fresh re-assertion of Suriname's claim over the New River area. This assertion was supported by the call for the expulsion of the 2,000 Guyanese resident in Suriname and threats of military action, despite unavailability of the TRIS units.[39]

After Pengel's displays of belligerence, the Vice-Premier and Minister of Realm Affairs of the Kingdom of the Netherlands, Dr Johannes Bakker, informed Pengel that there was no way that either Dutch troops or the TRIS would become involved in the territorial controversy as, in his words 'There are sufficient means for settling the dispute peacefully.' For Pengel, it meant that the reasonably well-equipped, and undoubtedly well-trained TRIS would be unavailable to support his ambitions and to bolster his political stock. His efforts to establish a network of airfields, supported by hydro-electric work in the area, was halted by the GPF.

Pengel then moved in an extremely dangerous direction with the creation of a special, heavily armed police unit, under the command of Major Sjoerd Lapré called DEFPOL (Defence Police). This unit had some 200 volunteers (mostly policemen and ex-TRIS soldiers) and was lightly armed with Uzi submachine guns, M1 carbines and second-hand khaki uniforms, all taken from TRIS stocks.[40] This unit, operating under Pengel's direction would be at the forefront of Suriname's ill-advised and unnecessary operations in the New River Triangle. Unfortunately, political expediency prevailed over good sense and a wholly unnecessary incident was precipitated to Suriname's overall detriment.

Initially, DEFPOL established four camps, the most formidable of which was a jungle fortress located on the eastern bank of the New River called Camp Tigri. One encounter led to the capture of nine GDF soldiers who were handed over to the TRIS and later repatriated. Suriname also made efforts to construct an airstrip in the vicinity of the camp and work was well underway when things took a turn for the worse as far as Suriname was concerned.

Budgetary issues came to the fore and three of the four Surinamese camps were subsequently shut down. Major Sjoerd Lapré was retired and Pengel's shaky administration collapsed in March 1969, when a transitional, ineffective regime led by Arthur May, a former civil servant, took office. This, combined with rioting and unrest in the Dutch colony of Curacao, convinced the Guyanese government of Forbes Burnham that the time was right to reclaim the disputed area. The airstrip, as yet unfinished at Camp Tigri, and which had been under Guyanese aerial surveillance from Guyana Defence Force Air Corps Helio Couriers, became an unexpected asset for the Guyanese as they undertook to force a decisive conclusion to their ongoing tensions with Suriname. Indeed, the inability of Suriname to support its interests in the theatre of operations was to prove costly.

Operation Climax remains one of the most daring and impressive operations mounted by any force within the English-speaking Caribbean. At its core was an extraordinary airborne assault operation undertaken by the GDF with assistance from

Display of GDF weapons including a 73mm SPG-9 recoilles rifle and an 82mm mortar. (GDF)

Guyana Airways whose Chief Pilot, Roland da Silva was convinced that the airline's De Havilland Canada Twin Otters could land on the unfinished Surinamese airstrip at Camp Tigri. This plan received the approval of Forbes Burnham and four Guyana Airways pilots – Roland da Silva, Michael Chan-A-Sue, Philip Jardim and Anthony Mekdeci – were commissioned as Majors in the GDF in preparation for this ambitious operation. Philip Jardim was to recall:

> In the 3 weeks leading up to the day we trained almost daily and soon gained absolute confidence in the performance capabilities of the Twin Otter which far outstripped de Havilland Canada's performance claims for it. We determined that we could land a fully laden Twin Otter and stop within 100 yards – 300 feet!! We could then take off an empty aircraft within 300 to 500 feet. We estimated that we had a distance of 600 feet but the only unknown was the surface bearing strength of the strip. However, the fact that it could support a Caterpillar D-4 bulldozer made us confident that we had nothing to fear – the one real unknown would be braking action.[41]

The GDF, now led by Colonel Clarence Price, prepared an operation led by the 1st Battalion commanded by Lieutenant Colonel Robert Stephenson. The force comprised some 45 GDF personnel from the 1 and 2 Companies of the 1st Battalion. Captain Martin Nascimento commanded No. 1 company; Captain Asad Ishoof, No. 2 company; Lieutenant Harry Hinds, leading the mortar platoon with 81mm mortars, and Lieutenant Marcus Munroe, the Reconnaissance Platoon – all being professional soldiers.

The two aircraft formation was led by an armed Twin Otter which had holes cut in its nose area for machine guns as well as observers. As Jardim was to note:

> Roland was flying the long-nosed Twin Otter with Michael Chan-A-Sue. This aircraft had had its nose dome removed and 4 holes cut in the fibreglass bulkhead for a GPMG (General Purpose Machine Gun), with the remaining 3 for sighting. W/O Hartley Liverpool – a large man, was seated in the nose with his belt-fed machine gun. I was flying the short-nosed Twin Otter with Tony Mekdeci. We were all armed with Sterling submachine guns. The cabin doors of both aircraft had been removed to enable the swift disembarkation of the troops, Roland would make the first approach, as his gunner could clear the potential machine gun nests I had noticed in the trees lining the strip. As soon as he was airborne again, I would land and he would cover me with his machine gunner.[42]

In the first phase of Operation Climax each aircraft took off with 22 armed soldiers on board. On landing, the soldiers disembarked while the aircraft were still moving and, as soon as the last soldier had disembarked, the aircraft got airborne once again. The GDF troops then cleared the airstrip of obstacles and secured it from retaliatory action. A party of Surinamese DEFPOL troops noticed the aircraft but were driven off by machine gun fire from W/O Liverpool's GPMG.[43]

The operation against Camp Tigri began with a mortar barrage from the mortars under Lieutenant Hinds. This convinced the DEFPOL personnel that they were outgunned. The GDF troops moved quickly through the jungle and fired at the building tops of the Surinamese camp to encourage the Surinamese to either surrender or depart. In the end, the Surinamese abandoned the camp and fled to the waterside and their boats and returned to Suriname, with one Surinamese DEFPOL soldier being taken prisoner but later repatriated. The Guyanese returned to the area with reinforcements, effectively dominating the area and renaming Camp Tigri as Camp Jaguar.[44]

This combat experience proved that the GDF was a capable and innovative force and capable of responding rapidly to an emerging situation. Unfortunately, as hinted before, Guyana's history of racial violence and politics was to prove to be a major factor in the GDF's development.

Race, Politics and Guyana's Security Forces: A Dangerous Mix

As Guyana's politics are dominated by race, with the two main racial groups being decidedly antagonistic towards each other, Guyana's security forces have found themselves embroiled in some degree of controversy. As has been discussed, the Guyana Defence Force (GDF) has its roots in the British Guyana Volunteer Force (BGVF) and in a Special Service Unit (SSU) established under the 1961–1964 Jagan administration. The BGVF was an overwhelmingly Afro-Guyanese outfit, but the SSU was established as a more representative entity with roughly equal numbers of Africans and Indians. In addition, the Guyanese police force was also an African dominated body.

However, between the years 1961 and 1964, the Jagan administration substantially increased the number of Indo-Guyanese recruited into the police force, perhaps in recognition of the spectre of racial violence that was haunting the country.[45] The low percentages of Indo-Guyanese in the police and BGVF were partly due to a certain Indian disinterest in joining such bodies because of the low pay and status, but also because of height and weight requirements that many Indians found difficult to meet. Furthermore, all recruiting was done almost exclusively by Africans and in urban areas where Indians did not live.[46]

In 1965, the International Commission of Jurists (ICJ) conducted an inquiry in which, among other things, the question of racial balance in the security forces was addressed. Their findings make interesting reading and indicate that Indians made up only 19.9 percent of the total security forces as shown in Table 10.[47]

The ICJ team recommended that there needed to be an increase in the number of Indians in the security forces. This, however, does not appear to have been implemented. As such, according to data released by the PPP, by 1973, Indo-Guyanese representation in the police force had fallen to 10 percent.[48] Table 11 seems to bear out the fact that Indo-Guyanese recruitment, based on information in Police Force Orders, seems to have been fallen in the years 1970 to 1977, most probably as part of a deliberate effort by the PNC to staff the security forces with its own supporters.[49] While this data is for the Guyana Police Force, it was replicated in the GDF.

The police in Guyana are a poorly paid and badly equipped group. Politicisation of the force during the PNC era, has also had a deleterious impact on discipline.[50] The Indo-Guyanese, after years of discrimination, have perhaps become somewhat unwilling to join such a force. The situation prevailing in the Guyana Defence Force is even worse. The SSU was a short-lived entity and the GDF that emerged from it rapidly became an overwhelmingly Afro-Guyanese body with minimal Indian participation. Despite having a few Indo-Guyanese officers, the GDF rapidly became the military arm of Forbes Burnham's PNC and was heavily involved in ballot-rigging between 1968 and 1992 and in human rights abuses against political opponents of the ruling party – largely, though by no means exclusively, Indo-Guyanese.

The PNC created a broad-based security structure that, at its peak, numbered over 21,000 men.[51] These were organised into a plethora of organisations and were very much under the control of the PNC. The two principal forces were, as might be expected, the police and the GDF. These, as has been shown, were overwhelmingly Afro-Guyanese in composition. Furthermore, it appears that following Dr Jagan's departure from power, there was a gradual purge of many of the Indo-Guyanese officers recruited during Dr Jagan's term.[52] The purges did not involve bloodshed, but many were passed over for promotion and frustrated career-wise. In the police, however, there appears to have been relatively little discrimination as far as Indo-Guyanese promotion was concerned, though, as has been shown, they were heavily discriminated against in recruitment.[53]

At the time of Burnham's death in 1985, the GDF had a strength of 7,000 personnel and was between 90 and 95 percent African in composition as far as the officer corps was concerned, and more than 85 percent African in the enlisted ranks.[54] The GDF was used as a means of providing unemployed PNC supporters and activists with steady wages.[55] The PPP and its Indo-Guyanese supporters were frequently harassed by the GDF which was routinely used to confiscate ballot boxes during the fraudulent elections held every five years and frequently patrolled villages dominated by Indo-Guyanese; one such incident in 1973 led to the deaths of Jagan Ramessar and Bholanauth Paramanand when they tried to stop ballot boxes from being stolen by the GDF to facilitate rigging by the PNC.[56]

The other two units: the Guyana People's Militia (GPM), which peaked at a strength of 3,000, and the Guyana National Service (GNS), which attained

Table 10: Racial balance of Guyanese security forces in 1965

	African	Indian	European	Portuguese	Mixed	Other
Police Force	2,122	710	7	28	149	45
Volunteer Force	507	51	6	4	3	3
Special Service Unit	72	72	0	0	2	0
Total	2,701	833	13	32	154	48
Percentage	73.5	19.9	0.3	0.8	4.2	1.3

Table 11: Racial composition of Guyanese security forces, 1970–1977

Year	Africans	Indians	Total Recruited
1970	160	3	163
1971	188	14	202
1972	210	20	230
1973	241	45	286
1974	299	40	339
1975	426	12	438
1976	276	17	293
1977	421	36	457
Total	2,221	187	2,408

a maximum strength of 4,500, were established as part of making Guyana more confident and self-sufficient, but rapidly became mere appendages of the ruling PNC. Service in the GNS was mandatory for men and women entering tertiary education, but intense distrust of the PNC operators of the scheme meant that many Guyanese opted out and chose to go to university abroad wherever possible. Both the GPM and GNS were roughly 90 percent African in composition and were another useful avenue for the employment of PNC activists and supporters. Two other units – the 2,000 strong National Guard service, and the 2,000 strong Young Socialist Movement (the youth arm of the PNC) were also created. Both groups were armed with military standard weapons and used on occasion to terrorise opponents of the PNC.[57]

Unfortunately, decades later, the spectres of race and political affiliation loom large over the GDF and the Guyanese security forces in general. While the security forces, faced with economic realities, were reduced in size to approximately 2,500 soldiers and 3,000 police, the ethnic imbalance continues, and efforts were made to analyse why this was the case.

In May 2004, Guyana's Disciplined Forces Commission submitted its final report, a year after it was constituted. The Commission's report dealt with, inter alia, measures to increase the efficacy of the Disciplined Forces as well as addressing the ethnic imbalance issue that has long plagued the Guyanese protective services. Of particular interest were the details released on the ethnic composition of the Guyana Defence Force (GDF) and the Guyana Police Force (GPF). In testimony before the Commission, the GDF indicated that it had, in 2003, an actual strength of some 2,630 personnel – 20 short of its authorised strength. Of these, 80 percent were Afro-Guyanese, 8 percent Indo-Guyanese and 12 percent other races.[58] The GPF was considerably less forthcoming with raw data about its composition and the Commission was forced to accept an observation that the 2,750 strong GPF seemed to have a ratio of one Indo-Guyanese officer to five non-Indo-Guyanese.[59]

While Guyana has avoided the intense race riots of the 1960s and 1970s, and the conduct of its elections since 1992 has been generally free and fair, if not always free from fear, the 2020 elections, as noted, saw a blatant attempt at rigging by the Granger regime. Ultimately, the PPP won, aided by efforts from the international community.

However, of great importance was a public statement from the GDF acting Chief of Staff, Brigadier Godfrey Bess, that the GDF is 'trained to support the democratically elected government of the day based on our constitution and that we will continue to do.'[60] Bess later pledged the GDF's support to the incoming elected president, Dr Irfaan Ali, thus avoiding any suggestion of the GDF acting in a subversive manner and making a refreshing change from the 1960s and 1970s. The GDF has thus come a long way from its politicised legacy but today faces a severe crisis of capability.

The Guyana Defence Force Today

The Guyana Defence Force is a shadow of its former self and is in dire need of recapitalisation, in particular its air and naval units. The GDF has an approximate regular strength of 3,100 personnel with a reserve strength of over 1,600. While this is a far cry from its bloated strength of the 1970s and 1980s, it is significantly larger than the

GDF troops armed with G-3 assault rifles, and equipped with a tactical radio set, seen during an exercise. (GDF)

Mortar team of the GDF. (GDF)

force that existed in the early 2000s and reflects security concerns emanating from the increasingly belligerent Maduro regime in Venezuela. However, this has not been matched by an increase in combat effectiveness. The GDF is organised into the following units:

1st Infantry Battalion Group
2nd Infantry Battalion Group
Guyana People's Militia
31 Special Forces Squadron
21st Artillery Company
Engineer Battalion
Signals Corps
Defence Headquarters
Training Corps
Intelligence Corps
Coast Guard
Band Corps
Medical Corps
Air Corps

The role of the GDF has remained largely unchanged and is to:

Defend the territorial integrity of Guyana
Assist the civil power in the maintenance of law and order when required to do so
Contribute to the economic development of Guyana

The Guyana Defence Force has a high-quality officer corps educated to graduate and undergraduate levels and has shown itself capable of interpreting and understanding national values and interests as well as performing military functions. The lower ranks, however, suffer from a poor quality of primary and secondary education which has become a major challenge for Guyana's broader society. Nonetheless, the GDF is quite well regarded by its Caribbean counterparts and its army is deemed to be reasonably competent.

GDF Army

Today, the Guyana Defence Force Army has two infantry battalions, a security battalion, a special forces squadron, a support unit, and an artillery company.[61] One of the battalions is effectively a reserve battalion formed out of a resurrected Guyana People's Militia which now has a strength of over 1,600 personnel.[62]

During the 1980s, the Amawai, Roraima, Ireng and Takutu sectors were manned by the Guyana Defence Force, while the Kutari sector was manned by the then Guyana National Service. The GDF units were amalgamated in 1988 to form the 1st Infantry Battalion Group.[63] This Battalion forms the principal combatant arm of the GDF.

The 2nd Infantry Battalion Group (Reserve) comprises of a regular and a reserve element. The regular element is largely administrative and is made up of an HQ, based at Camp Ayanganna, the main training base at Seweyo, Linden Highway, and the 241 Rifle Company (based at Seweyo). The reserve contributes four reserve rifle companies, namely 242 Company (which covers Regions 4 and 5), 243 Company (Regions 2 and 3), 244 Company (Region 6) and 245 Company (Region 10).[64] The combat effectiveness of this reserve unit is still doubtful.

Infantry weapons are a mix of Western and ex-communist bloc with M60 and FN MAG machine guns serving alongside ex-Yugoslav M70s, Chinese Type 56 rifles, PKM machine guns and RPG-7 rocket launchers. No armoured vehicles have been observed in GDF army service, though a few are found with the GPF for anti-riot duty.

The 21st Artillery Company operates the remaining artillery systems, legacy weapons from the GDF's flirtation with the communist bloc. The 76mm ZiS-3 remains in service in small numbers alongside 107mm WZ-3 towed rocket launchers and 120mm mortars while the status of the twelve 122mm artillery pieces received from the DPRK is unknown. The sole air defences are provided by single and quad 14.5mm KPV machine guns, and 12.7mm machine guns usually used in a ground support role. A number of 81mm and 82mm mortars provide battalion level support for the two Infantry Battalion Groups of the GDF while a very limited anti-tank capability exists in the form of 73mm SPG-9 and 82mm Type 65 recoilless rifles.

Guyana Defence Force Air Corps

In 2019, the Air Corps had one Shorts Skyvan, two BN-2 Islanders, and one Y-12 for light transport duties. In addition, it operates two Bell 206B, one Bell 412 and one RotorWay Exec 162F helicopters, the latter being for training local pilots.

Thus, the GDF planned for the procurement of two additional Skyvans and of two BN-2 Islanders in 2018. The Guyana Defence Force Air Corps took delivery of two second-hand Shorts SC.7 Skyvan aircraft – registration markings 8R-GWJ and 8R-GBW – at the end of June 2019, completing a recapitalisation process that also saw the acquisition of two used Britten-Norman Islander aircraft.[65]

The two Islanders which arrived in August 2018 have remained grounded as inspections continue. An attempt to fly one of the Islanders was aborted when engine troubles emerged, calling into question the logic of procuring used aircraft from civil sources, in this case the Islanders having been operated by the Brazilian based Aero Star Táxi Aére.[66]

Further enhancements to the GDF Air Corps rotary wing assets include orders for two Bell 412EPI and two Bell 429 helicopters which would provide a modern, albeit small, helicopter force to the GDF Air Corps.[67] According to Latin American defence sources:

> The helicopter was acquired through the U.S. Department of State, as part of a purchase request that the Guyanese government made for four aircraft, two Bell 412EPI and two Bell 429, in addition to complementary equipment, training, and maintenance. The

Table 12: Aircraft of the GDF

Aircraft	Type	Versions	In service	Notes
Short Skyvan	Utility transport	SC-7 Skyvan 3M	3	In service since 1979
Harbin Y-12 Panda	STOL utility transport	Y-12	1	In service since 2002
Britten-Norman BN-2 Islander	Utility transport	BN-2	2	In service since 2018
Bell 206 JetRanger	Utility helicopter	206B	2	In service since 1976
Bell 412	Utility helicopter	412SP	1	One on order
Bell 429	Utility	429	2	On order
RotorWay Exec 162F	Light helicopter	162F	1	In service since 2004

program's estimated cost is $256 million, the U.S. Defense Security Cooperation Agency said on its website. The U.S. government approved the overseas military sale in October 2020.[68]

The GDF Air Corps now has the modest strength of one Bell 412EPI helicopter, delivered in 2021,[69] (another being put up for sale as beyond recovery), two Bell 206B-3 helicopters, one Chinese Y-12 transport aircraft which has been undergoing repairs for some time, two Shorts SC.7 Skyvans, two grounded BN-2 Islanders and a Cessna 206 seized from narcotics traffickers, which has not been put into service.

The GDF has also sought a single UAV but this has not yet materialised and it is unclear as to what new procurements will be undertaken by the PPP government. Of particular note is the absence of maritime patrol aircraft.

Guyana Coast Guard

To call the Guyana Defence Force Coast Guard underequipped would be a massive understatement. The sole ocean-going craft remains the GDFS *Essequibo*, formerly the Royal Navy River-class minesweeper, HMS *Orwell*. This ageing vessel is in dire need of repair and refit if it is to continue in service. At present it is unserviceable and one Guyanese press report noted:

> Once the flagship vessel, the converted British minesweeper, GDFS Essequibo formerly HMS *Orwell*, which was acquired in 2001 has been rendered unserviceable and so the army does not have any vessels that can patrol at certain distances and depths of the Exclusive Economic Zone.[70]

The Coast Guard has one Kimbala-class landing craft. Its other assets are eight T-44 motor lifeboats used as patrol craft and seven Metal Shark vessels – two 38ft craft and five 28ft craft. The latter vessels are the Coast Guard's most modern fast patrol vessels but are fit for use primarily as interceptors as they lack the endurance, sensor suite and armament to serve in any more demanding task.

These vessels are supplemented by GPF vessels, the most notable of which is the MV *Baramani* and a fisheries monitoring vessel *Cavalli* which is operated by the Department of Fisheries. Both of these vessels are of dubious utility and the GDF Coast Guard is in dire need of re-equipment, especially with the increasing demands of offshore oil installations needing some degree of protection and the absence of suitable assets.

To this end, the GDF has sought assistance from the United States to bolster its assets with additional Metal Shark vessels seemingly being sought. It is unclear as to whether Guyana has been offered any decommissioned US Coast Guard vessels of the Island-class or any smaller vessels. However, it should be noted that Guyana's Coast Guard manpower is at present very limited and training any substantial or effective cadre of seagoing personnel will take some time. It is known that the Dutch company Damen shipbuilders has offered a combination of SPa 4207 and FCS 5009 vessels to Guyana but, to date, nothing has materialised.

Conclusion

The Guyana Defence Force is in an interesting situation where the country is on the cusp of financial prosperity on a scale that the country has not seen before. This may not immediately translate into new equipment for the GDF but with more money available and an increasing threat from Venezuela, there is no doubt that the force needs new equipment, especially in respect of its maritime and air assets. Whether this will materialise will depend on the political imperatives of the new government which has to balance numerous priorities. Nonetheless, the GDF, now free from its heavily politicised past, has every reason to feel hopeful that new equipment will materialise.

5
JAMAICA

Background

Jamaica is the largest of the islands in the English-speaking Caribbean and is also the most populous. Jamaica is some 10,990 square kilometres (4,240 square miles) in area and it is the third largest island of the Greater Antilles and the Caribbean (after Cuba and Hispaniola). The country lies about 145 kilometres (90 miles) south of Cuba, and 191 kilometres (119 miles) to the west of Hispaniola which is the island that contains the two countries of Haiti and the Dominican Republic. Some 215 kilometres (134 miles) to the north-west is the British Overseas Territory of the Cayman Islands.

Of Jamaica's 2.97 million people, Jamaicans of African descent represent 76.3 percent of the population, followed by 15.1 percent Afro-European, 3.4 percent East Indian and Afro-East Indian, 3.2 percent Caucasian, 1.2 percent Chinese and 0.8 percent other racial groups.[1] The country's religious demographic is dominated by Christianity (65 percent Protestant, 2 percent Catholic) with over 20 percent of the population declaring that they follow no religion. The country is relatively poor but has a high human development index though there are substantial income disparities which lead to conflict and at times violent unrest, especially during periods of economic decline or uncertainty.

Jamaica's economy is dominated by the service sector, which accounts for 70 percent of the GDP. There is a vibrant tourism sector centred around a number of coastal resorts, insulated from the crime prone urban areas and hinterland of the country. The country has a substantial bauxite industry which at one stage was the mainstay of the economy and the country is a major producer of both bauxite and alumina. In addition, the country has sought to encourage foreign investment and garment manufacturing which contribute significantly to the economy. Jamaica has a considerable agricultural sector, with sugar cane and bananas being its primary crops.

Jamaica is different from Trinidad and Tobago and Guyana in that, despite its extremely violent society, it has had a somewhat more peaceful internal political situation, though political violence and electoral fraud was not unknown in Jamaica. While Jamaica's criminal gangs indulge in considerable violence, Jamaica has not seen Trinidad's military mutiny and Islamist insurrection and has not faced the vicious ethnic violence and brutally racist politics of Guyana. Jamaica's challenges are more typical of a country facing the

Two decommissioned Ferret armoured cars of the JDF serving as gate guardians in Kingston. (JDF)

combined challenges of poverty and organised crime inspiring gang violence with a ready supply of narcotics and weapons.

The Jamaica Defence Force – Mission and Overview

'To provide military capability to deter and or defeat threats against the Jamaican state and or its interests'.[2]

The Jamaica Defence Force is a brigade-sized unit comprising land, sea and air formations and is possibly the largest military establishment within the English-speaking Caribbean. Dating back to 1962, the Jamaica Defence Force has its roots in the West India Regiment which lasted between 1795 and 1926 and thereafter as the military force of the West Indies Federation which existed between 1958 and 1962. The JDF was formed out of the 1st Battalion of the West India Regiment and was later supplemented by small air and naval components. The JDF enjoys a good reputation within the West Indies, having a high standard of training and discipline and compared to the military establishments in other West Indian islands, has maintained an organisational stability that has stood it in good stead over the last five decades.

The JDF has primarily been used to reinforce the Jamaica Constabulary Force (JCF), which is the island's police force, in internal security operations which have been known to degenerate into pitched battles against well-armed criminal gangs. One of the more recent, and certainly most notorious incidents being the 2010 operations against the 'Shower Posse' drug gang in an attempt to arrest its leader Christopher 'Dudus' Coke. These operations saw the JDF and JCF engaged in urban combat with some 500 armed gang members in which four security personnel and 73 civilians lost their lives. The JDF deployed APCs and helicopters in support of its operations while the JCF employed weapons up to and including anti-materiel rifles to neutralise gang gun positions. The JDF was also deployed in support of the JCF in 1999 and 2001 to deal with extensive unrest sparked through an explosive combination of economic hardship, violent political agitation, and well-armed criminal gangs.

The Jamaica Constabulary Force has a strength of between 11,000 and 12,000 personnel, well-armed with a combination of assault rifles, submachine guns and semi-automatic pistols and a small number of .50 calibre Barrett M82 anti-materiel rifles. In addition to its not inconsiderable firepower, the JCF's Special Operations Branch – formerly called the Mobile Reserve – and its SWAT team operate a number of Lenco Bearcat armoured vehicles which have proved to be invaluable during operations against the country's heavily armed gangs. The extent of the challenge faced by the JCF can be seen by the fact that at least one JCF armoured vehicle was successfully attacked and severely damaged. The JCF is increasingly a partner of the JDF during internal security operations. The JCF intends to increase its number of personnel to 18,000 by 2024, making it by far the largest police force in the English-speaking Caribbean.[3] However, the JCF has been plagued by reports of criminality in its ranks, extra-judicial killings and endemic corruption, and though strenuous efforts have been made to improve the JCF, it lacks the required professionalism to handle Jamaica's challenges without help from the more professional JDF.

Despite its undoubted professionalism, the JDF suffers from the bane of all military establishments in the English-speaking Caribbean – poor maintenance. Inadequate maintenance and a failure to procure spares in a timely manner have resulted in the demise of the JDF's Ferret Scout Cars (which now serve as gate guardians), the Air Wing's AS.355, Bell 212 and UH-1 helicopters as well as its Beech King Air and Cessna 210 aircraft, with its two BN-2A Islanders being barely operable. The Jamaica Coast Guard barely puts to sea and while it nominally has six patrol boats on strength, is practically without operational assets. Of great concern to the JDF was its inability to keep its ageing force of fourteen V-150 APCs serviceable. Given the fact that these vehicles have proven invaluable in protecting JDF personnel during urban operations, their replacement became of considerable urgency. Similarly, the Coast Guard urgently needed to restore capability. To this end a limited re-equipment programme for the JDF has started and will be discussed in detail.

Beyond its internal security role, the JDF saw service in Grenada between 1983 and 1985 in the aftermath of Operation Urgent Fury as part of the Caribbean Peace Force – along with forces from Barbados and police Special Service Units from the Organisation of Eastern Caribbean States. It has also served in Haiti as part of a joint

A Ferret armoured car and a jeep mounting a Browning M1919 machine gun, both belonging to the Jamaica Regiment. (JDF)

CARICOM Battalion. The JDF maintains very close ties with the British military and joint exercises are a routine occurrence which has served to preserve a high degree of professionalism in the JDF and its officers are held in high esteem within the Caribbean.

The professionalism of the JDF, besides its armed capacity, has been demonstrated during humanitarian relief missions to disaster affected islands. Jamaica's ability and willingness to respond to calls for assistance has made the JDF an important regional asset in times of crisis. Its training facilities are also in demand and many countries send their officer cadets to train at Jamaican establishments. The country also houses the academically accredited, Caribbean Military Academy which was formed in May 2019.

The Jamaica Defence Force History: 1962 to 2005

The Jamaica Defence Force traces its origins to the seventeenth century and has a rich history prior to 1962. The JDF might be able to trace its roots to the Jamaica Militia of 1662. This was the military organisation that was formed after the conquest of Jamaica by the troops of England's Oliver Cromwell in 1655. The Militia successfully fended off the only subsequent invasion of the island in 1694 when a force of 1,400 French troops were repulsed by Militia at Carlisle Bay in southern Clarendon.[4] The Militia remained the primary military force on the island until 1906, peaking during the Napoleonic Wars with 18 regiments of infantry – one for each Parish – and three of cavalry – being on hand during the nineteenth century.[5]

Jamaican soldiers served in both world wars, as part of the Kingston Infantry Volunteers in the First World War and the Jamaica Infantry Volunteers in the Second World War. As part of the Jamaica Battalion and as part of West Indian troops assigned to British Forces, Jamaican soldiers served in several theatres during the conflict although combat duties were relatively limited. A West India Regiment, tracing its ancestry to 1888 also existed for many years, and fought as battalions during the First World War before being disbanded in January 1927.[6]

Between the years 1958 and 1962, the English-speaking Caribbean attempted to forge a political union called the West Indies Federation. This was comprised of the ten English-speaking territories of Antigua and Barbuda, Barbados, Dominica, Grenada, Jamaica, Montserrat, the then St Kitts-Nevis-Anguilla, St Lucia, St Vincent, and Trinidad and Tobago. The West Indies Federation was legislatively established by the British Caribbean Federation Act of 1956 and had the aim of establishing a political union among its members.[7] The Federation was a courageous experiment and was a recognition of the small size and lack of viability of the smaller islands as independent states. However, a referendum in Jamaica in 1961 in favour of withdrawing from the Federation and declaring independence led to the collapse of the Federation with Jamaica and Trinidad becoming independent countries and the others following over the next decade, though most remained members of the Commonwealth with Governors-General as their respective heads of state.

The military arm of the Federation was a resurrected West India Regiment which amalgamated the Jamaica Battalion (now renamed the Jamaica Regiment) with other units into a force that was to grow to three infantry battalions – one based in Jamaica, one in Trinidad and the other a composite unit nominally based in Barbados.[8]

The West India Regiment was officially reformed on 1 January 1959, by absorbing the greater part of the Jamaica Regiment. The Jamaica Regiment's personnel were transferred to the new WIR which was headquartered in Jamaica at Harman Barracks in Kingston. Later, in September, it was decided to raise a second battalion of the WIR with an aim of bringing the initial strength of the regiment to 1,640, with a total of 730 soldiers for each of the Jamaica and Trinidad battalions.[9]

One year later, in 1960, the 1st Battalion of the WIR was organised as a basic rifle battalion along British lines – four companies, one of which was a headquarters company and had a depot with administrative staff. Its personnel strength comprised some 500 men, half of whom were Jamaican, plus about 40 seconded British officers and men. As befitting a pan-West Indian unit, the proportion of non-Jamaicans in the battalion increased to two-thirds of the establishment during 1960 and 1961 but the majority of the officers remained Jamaicans.[10] The 2nd Battalion, based in Trinidad, was formed as planned in 1960, as was a 3rd Battalion which recruited more widely. In anticipation of and in preparation for eventual West Indian independence, some military installations and bases previously used only by the British army were transferred to the WIR. These included Newcastle which in 1959 became the Federal Defence Force Training Depot and was tasked with training recruits from all over the newly formed Federation of the West Indies.[11]

As with other regional institutions, the West India Regiment was to promote a sense of shared heritage and common pride and, as such, would be recruited from the various islands. By September 1961, in addition to the Jamaicans, about 200 Trinidadians were serving in the regiment, with 14 Antiguans and 12 from St Kitts and Nevis.

A Cadillac V-150 armoured car of the Jamaica Regiment. (JDF)

However, as a pan-Caribbean unit, the WIR met with the same fate as the West Indies Federation and collapsed with the 1st Battalion becoming the foundation of the Jamaica Regiment and the Jamaica Defence Force. The 2nd Battalion was, with some effort, turned into a viable foundation for the Trinidad and Tobago Regiment (TTR) and Trinidadian personnel serving with the WIR were given a choice to serve with either the JDF or the TTR. Some chose to serve with the JDF for a few years before returning to Trinidad.

It should also be noted that despite the proliferation of islands and the attendant maritime challenges facing the English-speaking Caribbean, the West India Regiment was a ground combat unit. Though a Caribbean Defence Force with a Coast Guard was planned, it never materialised.

The JDF was thus formed out of a combination of a proud military lineage and a more recent effort at a unified regional military force. It was eventually formally established in 1962, as Jamaica emerged as an independent country on 6 August 1962. Its post-independence history is summarised officially as follows:

> The Jamaica Defence Force (JDF) was formed on 31 July 1962 with the West India Regiment – disbanded just the day before – providing the nucleus. On formation, the Force comprised two regular units 'Headquarters and Support Units' (colloquially known as "Staff and Services"), and the First Battalion The Jamaica Regiment (1JR), as well as the Jamaica National Reserve, at that time comprising one infantry battalion.
>
> The Third Battalion The Jamaica Regiment (3JR(NR)), which was formed in 1961 as the then sole component of the Jamaica National Reserve, became a part of the Jamaica Defence Force on 31 July 1962. Headquarters and Support Units comprised the Force Headquarters, the Garrison Administrative Unit, the Jamaica Military Stores Depot, the Jamaica Military Workshop, the Military Estates Office and the Jamaica Military Pay and Records Office. In 1963 the Jamaica Air Wing, the Jamaica Sea Squadron and the Force Engineer Unit (incorporating the Military Estates Office) were formed as sub-units of Headquarters and Support Units.
>
> The Jamaica Military Band (the band of the original West India Regiment of 1795 which, following the regiment's disbanding, had been renamed 'Jamaica Military Band' in 1927 with semi-military status) had become a purely civilian unit in 1959 as a corporate body under the Ministry of Home Affairs. It now became a part of the Jamaica Defence Force with the advent of Independence in 1962.[12]

However, this official synopsis hardly does justice to a force which had, from its inception, been the senior military unit of the English-speaking Caribbean and which, from the outset, served as a model for other armed forces within the region.

The Jamaica Regiment

In the aftermath of the disbanding of the West Indies Regiment and the collapse of the Federation, the 1st Battalion and 3rd Battalion of the latter became the 1st Battalion and 3rd Battalion of the Jamaica Regiment respectively. The 2nd Battalion was to become the nucleus of the Trinidad and Tobago Regiment. In the prelude to independence, the Jamaica Local Forces (JLF) were formed as one of the conditions under which Jamaica was granted independence. The JLF was to eventually become the Jamaica Defence Force and its component land, sea and air elements, the latter two being very modest to start, were tasked with the following duties:[13]

Defence against military or paramilitary threats
Military aid to Civil Authorities
Internal Security Support
Counter-narcotics Operations
Search and Rescue (SAR) Operations
Humanitarian and disaster relief
Counterterrorism
State ceremonials

A Bushmaster of the Protected Mobility Suqadron, Jamaica Regiment. (JDF)

Troops of the Jamaica Regiment on mobile patrol. (JDF)

For decades, the Jamaica Regiment had two regular infantry battalions – the 1st Battalion The Jamaica Regiment and the 2nd Battalion The Jamaica Regiment – which rotated their deployment between the Lathbury Barracks, located at Up Park Camp, Kingston and the Moneague Training Camp, Moneague, St Ann. This rotation is usually done at the beginning of each year and allows for familiarisation of each unit.[14]

Both battalions were tasked with assisting the Jamaica Constabulary Force (JCF) in maintaining law and order in designated areas which are deemed to warrant military deployment. To this end, a Joint Task Force Headquarters comprising command elements from both the JCF and the JDF was established and functions to date.

The senior unit of the Jamaica Regiment is the 1st Battalion The Jamaica Regiment (1JR) and was formed on the 31 July 1962. Formed with an initial strength of four rifle companies, a support company and a headquarters company. However, by 1979 the Battalion had grown to eight companies and was becoming administratively unwieldy.[15]

By the late 1970s there was an acceptance that a second regular infantry battalion was needed. The 1970s saw a good deal of electoral violence in Jamaica and the JDF was heavily committed to supporting the JCF in trying to keep political violence to within manageable levels. In May the Battalion was split in two.

Four companies remained as the 1st Battalion The Jamaica Regiment while the other four companies were used to form the 2nd Battalion The Jamaica Regiment, whose home base became the Moneague Training Camp in St Ann. Thus, on 21 May 1979 the 2nd Battalion The Jamaica Regiment (2JR) mustered for the first time in the men's dining hall at the Moneague Training Camp in St Ann and was in action within a few weeks in disaster relief operations during heavy flooding in 1979.[16]

The Jamaica Regiment's reserve formation was, until recently, the 3rd Battalion of the Jamaica Regiment. Formally designated as the 3rd Battalion The Jamaica Regiment (National Reserve), the personnel of the unit, after undergoing initial training, are only required to serve a minimum of 19 days in each year, thus allowing people with regular employment to serve in the military. The National Reserve has four barracks across Jamaica: Curphey Barracks – Up Park Camp; Foster Barracks – Mandeville; Burke Barracks – Montego Bay; and Whitehorne Barracks – Port Maria.[17] As befitting its major encampment, Up Park Camp houses the 3rd Battalion's headquarters, the Headquarter Company, and two rifle companies, 'Alpha' and 'Bravo'. As might be expected for reserve formations, each of the rifle companies is headed by a Training Major while the Regular Force provides a cadre of senior NCOs for the National Reserve.[18]

The equipment available to the Jamaica Regiment was almost exclusively of British origin until the 1990s. The main battle rifle was the 7.62mm L1A1 SLR rifle, with the Sterling submachine gun, FN MAG general purpose machine gun, 51mm mortars and M79 grenade launcher rounding out the infantry weapons issued at section, platoon and company level. Battalion fire support is centred around 81mm L16 mortars.

Unlike the armed forces of other islands of the English-speaking Caribbean (not including Guyana), the Jamaica Regiment invested in a force of armoured vehicles early in its history with a small number of Ferret armoured cars – perhaps as many as 15 – being available even in the early years of its formation. Unlike the two Dingo armoured cars available to the Trinidad and Tobago Regiment, Jamaica's Ferrets were fully operational vehicles, intended for internal security operations. These armoured cars were armed with machine guns but it is unclear how long they were retained in service as they were likely to be second-hand Ferret Mk.4s and as such had been heavily used before delivery to Jamaica in the 1960s.

The Commando Squadron of the Royal Bahamas Defence Force acquired two Shaanxi Baoji Tiger 4x4 APCs from China in 2017. They have a crew of two, can carry eight or nine passengers and provide protection against small arms. (Artwork by David Bocquelet)

Between the 1970s and 2012, the Jamaica Regiment acquired a total of 15 Cadillac-Gage V-150 Commando armoured cars. Most had a machine gun turret for a 7.62x51mm general-purpose machine gun. After years of low serviceability, they have been replaced by the Bushmasters. (Artwork by David Bocquelet)

The Protected Mobility Vehicle Squadron of the Jamaica Regiment now operates 12 Bushmasters, with 6 more on order. The vehicles acquired from Thales Australia wear a three-tone paint scheme, can carry nine passengers in addition to the driver and can be armed with a pintle-mounted machine gun. (Artwork by David Bocquelet)

The Royal Bahamas Defence Force operates a fleet of four Damen SPa 3007s for coastal patrol duties. All are painted grey overall, have a minimal sensor suite, and no permanently installed armament other than mounts for machine guns. The vessel is shown flying the Dutch flag during its trials in The Netherlands. (Artwork by David Bocquelet)

The Barbados Defence Force Coast Guard operates a force of three Damen SPa 4207 patrol vessels. Now in service for 20 years, they are modestly equipped with surveillance gear and have mountings for machine gun, and fire monitor installed forward. (Artwork by David Bocquelet)

The Jamaica Defence Force Coast Guard has ordered two Damen FCS 5009 vessels for utility, long-range patrol, and search and rescue tasks. One has now been delivered and named *Nanny of the Maroons*. It has mountings for machine guns but no permanently installed armament. A rescue boat and a crane are installed aft. Two similar, but slightly modified vessels are operated by the Trinidad and Tobago Coast Guard: they have GAM-BO1 20mm automatic cannon as their primary armament. (Artwork by David Bocquelet)

The Trinidad and Tobago Coast Guard operates four Damen SPa 5009 vessels. These are well-equipped ships with a comprehensive surveillance suite, including a Kelvin Hughes Sharp-Eye radar and a FLIR-system. Each has a 7.5m RHIB launched via the stern, and a Damen DI 1102 Interceptor boat launched with help of a davit. As well as machine gun mounts, they are armed with the Rheinmetal/MSI Seahawk LW20A1 remotely controlled weapon system including a 20mm automatic cannon. (Artwork by David Bocquelet)

The Jamaica Defence Force Air Wing is in the process of taking delivery of nine Bell 429 helicopters, planned to replace remaining Bell 407s and Bell 412s in service. New 429s are all equipped with an integrated surveillance system made by the CNC Technologies, and are all painted in dark green overall. (Artwork by Pablo Albornoz)

Between 2011 and 2012, the Trinidad and Tobago Air Guard took delivery of four Agusta-Westland AW.139 helicopters. All are painted as shown here, in dark sea grey and dark green overall, and wear the recently introduced roundels, including a hummingbird in its centre. Well-equipped with searchlights, FLIR-turrets, a rescue winch, and the capacity to carry fire-fighting equipment, following a bizarre and untimely grounding in 2017, they never achieved fully-operational status. Even though maintained in airworthy condition, all four have been withdrawn from service: only one is sporadically flown, even if not certified for use. (Artwork by Pablo Albornoz)

The Guyana Defence Force Air Corps operated Britten-Norman BN-2 Islander short-take-off and landing aircraft from 1971 until 1998. In 2018, it acquired two refurbished examples to replace them: though at least one has experienced ongoing severe engine difficulties. Since 2019, they may have been re-painted into military colours, instead of their civilian scheme shown here. (Artwork by Tom Cooper)

In addition to the Islanders, the Guyana Defence Corps used to operate Shorts Skyvan light transports. The first was acquired in 1979, and two refurbished examples were acquired as recently as in 2019, to augment the last survivor of earlier acquisitions. All are painted in dark green overall. (Artwork by Tom Cooper)

The sole maritime patrol aircraft operated by the Jamaica Defence Force Air Wing is a brand-new Beech King Air 350ER. This aircraft is equipped with modern radar and other advanced communications and surveillance equipment. Painted in ghost grey overall, it wears full Jamaican national markings and the service title, but only a civilian-style registration. (Artwork by Pablo Albornoz)

The Trinidad and Tobago Air Guard still operates two Fairchild C-26 light transports. One of these, serial number 216, has been modified through the installation of a FLIR-turret under the front fuselage, and an Israeli-made ELTA M-2022 radar in a dome under the rear fuselage. The second example, serial number 215, has no such equipment and is primarily deployed for transport purposes. Notably, both aircraft originally wore the TTAG crest and their serials only: the three-colour stripe (representing the country's national colours) and the full roundel have been applied only since 2013. (Artwork by Tom Cooper)

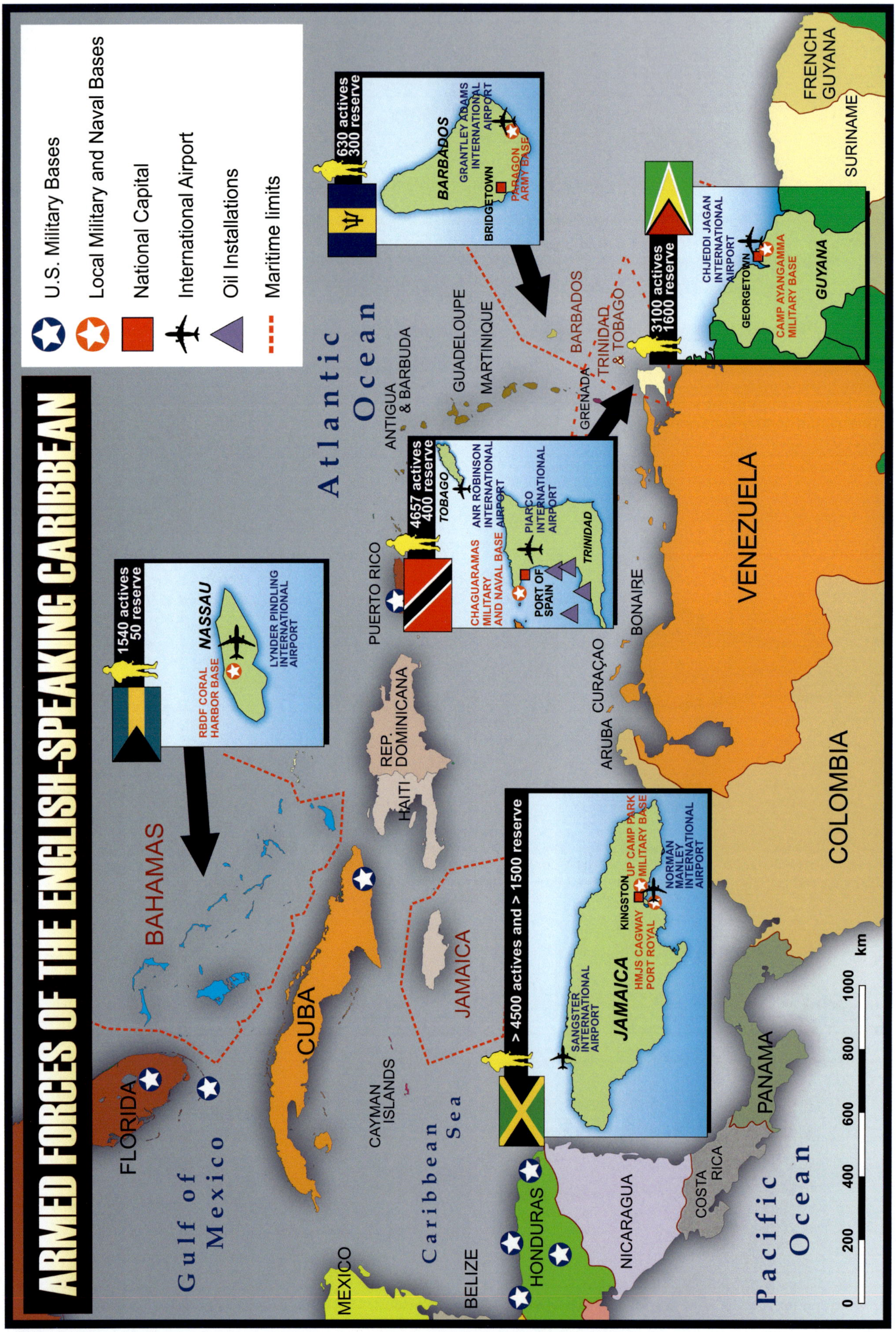

(Map by Anderson Subtil)

It is likely they were withdrawn in the 1970s.

The Ferrets augmented a force of machine gun armed trailer-trucks supplied by the United States but both the Ferrets and the machine gun trucks were supplemented and largely supplanted by a force of some 15 V-150 Cadillac Gage armoured personnel carriers.[19]

The latter vehicles were to become the mainstay of the Jamaica Regiment's protected mobility forces and saw extensive use during internal security operations from 1976 onwards. These vehicles were to prove particularly useful during the sporadic cycles of electoral violence to clear burning roadblocks as well as periods of urban unrest and violence, most recently in Tivoli Gardens in 2010.

Table 13: Legacy Aircraft used by the JDF Air Wing[24]

Aircraft Type	Quantity	Service Entry	Out of Service	Origin
Aerospatiale AS.355 Ecureuil	4	1999	2007	France
Beech A100 King Air	1	1975	2003	USA
Beech B60 Duke	1	1975	1981	USA
Bell 47G Sioux	2	1963	1971	USA
Bell 205A	4	1974	1975	USA
Bell 206 JetRanger	8	1971	current	USA
Bell 212 Twin Huey	3	1973	1998	USA
Bell 222UT	1	1986	1988	USA
Bell 407	4	2007	current	USA
Bell 412	3	1998	current	USA
Bell UH-1H Iroquois	4	1989	2002	USA
Britten-Norman BN-2A Islander	2	1974	2012	UK
Cessna 185 Skywagon	4	1963	1977	USA
Cessna 210 Centurion	3	1983	2011	USA
Cessna 337G (O-2A) Skymaster	1	1983	1994	USA
De Havilland Canada DHC-6 Twin Otter	1	1967	1978	Canada
Rockwell Commander 695A	1	2004	2006	ex-civil

The Jamaican Defence Force Air Wing

The Jamaican Defence Air Wing was formed in June 1963, initially as the Jamaican Air Squadron with pilots from the civilian Jamaican Flying Club. One month later the Jamaican Defence Force Air Wing was established on 3 July 1963 with the arrival of four Cessna 185s. These were later joined by a small force of two Bell 47G helicopters that were ferry-flown to Jamaica from Texas.[20]

Flying training was carried out in England until 1972 and after that in Canada, but Jamaica has made strenuous efforts to develop an indigenous training capability. From 1971 to 1973, the Air Wing received some Bell 206 and Bell 212 helicopters. The former type was to become a major element in the Air Wing's operational and training inventory, with a single type continuing in service to date. The Bell 212s, three of which were delivered in 1973, lasted in service until 1998 when they were withdrawn from use.[21]

In April 1977 the Air Wing became an autonomous unit within the JDF but was still largely subordinated to the Jamaica Regiment. A number of light transport and liaison aircraft were procured from the 1970s onwards with the Britten-Norman BN-2 being the most effective of these assets. However, various Cessna light aircraft were to predominate in the Air Wing, these being principally tasked with light transport duties with some limited use in the maritime

Bell 407 and Bell 412 of the JDF Air Wing. (JDF)

A Diamond DA42 trainer of the JDF Air Wing. (JDF)

Bell 407s and Bell 429s of the JDF Air Wing. (JDF)

patrol role, though they were never equipped with any sensors fit for the task.[22]

A modernisation of the helicopter fleet took place during 1989 when four Bell UH-1Hs were leased from the US government. One of these crashed in 1997 with the other three being withdrawn from use and returned in 2002. In fact, most of the Air Wing's equipment was sold in the late 1980s and 1990s. A fresh start was made at the beginning of 2000 when the Air Wing was re-equipped with the Bell 412 and Aerospatiale AS.355 Ecureuil. The latter type lasted for only seven years in JDF service.[23]

Like the Jamaican Coast Guard, the JDF Air Wing was to receive a new lease of life in the mid-2000s and has received a good deal of new equipment in the form of new models of Bell helicopters, establishing a very strong relationship with the Bell company. However, its fixed wing assets have not received similar attention and have atrophied.

The Jamaica Coast Guard

The naval arm of the JDF was formed in 1963, one year after the formation of the JDF. This naval arm was called the 'Jamaica Sea Squadron' and was established with an initial complement of three 63ft wooden Second World War torpedo recovery boats provided by the United States government. These vessels were commissioned (Her Majesty's Jamaican Ship) HMJS *Yoruba* (P1), HMJS *Coromante* (P2) and HMJS *Mandingo* (P3). As was common with the English-speaking Caribbean, a training team from the Royal Navy assisted with the Sea Squadron's early development.[25]

Some four years later, the Sea Squadron was renamed the Jamaica Defence Force Coast Guard (JDF CG) in 1966. In the tradition of British inspired forces, a naval White Ensign, naval rank insignia and Royal Navy-pattern uniforms were adopted. It should be noted that the JDF Coast Guard nominally holds army ranks – similar to the Air Wing and the Jamaica Regiment. This reflects the relatively subordinate role of the Coast Guard to the Jamaica Regiment and its land forces. This would seem to be counter intuitive for an island nation, but Jamaica's terrestrial internal security challenges have meant a focus on land forces.

In 1966, the JDF Coast Guard got rid of its wholly inadequate 63-foot boats and acquired the first of three 85ft all aluminium Bay-class patrol boats. These vessels, HMJS *Discovery Bay* (P4), HMJS *Holland Bay* (P5) and HMJS *Manatee Bay* (P6), were commissioned between 1966 and 1967. The Bay-class vessels were modified

Two Damen SPa 4207s of the Jamaica Coast Guard, in the company of a Bell 412 of the JDF Air Wing. (JDF)

Two interceptors and two Damen SPa 4207s of the JDF Coast Guard. (JDF)

HMJS *Cornwall* and HMJS *Middlesex* – both of the SPa 4207 class – seen while returning to base. (JDF)

In 1974, the JDF Coast Guard acquired the first of two 'offshore' patrol vessels with HMJS *Fort Charles* (P7) being acquired. This vessel with a crew of 20 was 103ft long, displaced 103 tonnes and was armed with a 20mm gun and two .50 calibre M2HB guns. The *Fort Charles* was followed in 1985 by HMJS *Paul Bogle* (P8) which was similarly equipped.[27]

The ageing vessels of the Jamaican Coast Guard were augmented by two Point-class cutters, transferred in 1999 from the US Coast Guard – as part of a package given to several Caribbean countries – but these vessels do not appear to have served a very long time in Jamaican service. The smaller vessels of the JDF Coast Guard – Dauntless coastal patrol vessels and various interceptors – underwent several refits during the 1990s and early years of the twenty-first century.

Jamaica's principal patrol assets – the *Fort Charles* and the *Paul Bogle* – served for a long time but were increasingly obsolescent and refits produced diminishing returns. This led to their replacement in 2005–2006 by a fleet of modern Damen SPa4027 vessels. Nonetheless, the two ships remained in commission for decades though were of dubious serviceability.

Politics and Controversy – 1972 to 1980

In the 1970s and into the early 1980s Jamaica was plagued by intense political polarisation, some of it along ideological lines. Pro-Western elements were pitted against so-called pro-communist elements and with the ever-present threat of Cuban influence, a degree of political paranoia was present in the left-wing government of Prime Minister Michael Manley. These tensions manifested themselves in a

commercial cabin cruiser designs and lasted in service well into the 1990s, though were of dubious serviceability. *Holland Bay* (P5) lasted until 2003, with at least two refits being undertaken.[26]

series of coup plots, of varying levels of intensity. Manley's left-of-centre politics was inherently antagonistic to the pro-Western training and orientation of the Jamaican security establishment and political tensions between political parties and both the JDF and JCF were evident into the early 1980s.

Manley, in particular, reduced the level of military cooperation with the United States to minimal levels between 1972 and 1980 in accordance with the ideology of his People's National Party (PNP). The United States made no secret of its preference for the right-of-centre views of the Jamaica Labour Party (JLP) of Edward Seaga.

As far as the JDF was concerned, two alleged coup attempts were attributed to some of its personnel. The first was in 1976 when a JLP Senator, Pearnel Charles, and a former JDF officer, Peter Whittingham, were arrested for allegedly plotting a coup. However, evidence was minimal and the two were released.

Rather more serious was the arrest of 33 JDF officers and members of a right-wing party – the Jamaica United Front Party – on 22 June 1980. They were charged with plotting to commandeer two armoured cars and overthrow the Manley government after kidnapping him and killing the JDF Chief of Staff.[28]

These tensions and coup plots came to an end in 1980 when Manley was defeated by Edward Seaga in the 30 October 1980 elections and have not resurfaced despite Manley returning to power in 1989, chastened and somewhat more moderate in his views.

Urgent Fury – the JDF and the Caribbean Peacekeeping Force

The JDF had an important role to play during the 1983 US intervention in Grenada. Unlike Barbados, however, the JDF had little role in the planning or reconnaissance undertaken prior to the operation, and while Jamaica was supportive of the intervention, its government was not as proactive as the Eastern Caribbean States or Barbados in terms of organising or encouraging intervention in Grenada. However, once it was decided that a Caribbean Peacekeeping Force was to be sent to Grenada, the Jamaica Regiment was called upon to provide leadership and troops.

While Brigadier (promoted from Colonel for the role) Rudyard Lewis of Barbados was given the task as regional coordinator, Colonel Ken Barnes of the Jamaica Defence Force was given command of the Caribbean Peacekeeping Force. To the reinforced rifle platoon of the Barbados Defence Force, the one hundred policemen of the Barbados Police Force, and 50 assorted police personnel from other Caribbean islands, the Jamaica Regiment despatched a full rifle company of 120 personnel, a mortar section with two 81mm mortars and a medical section, giving a total of 150 JDF personnel being committed to Grenada, making it the only fully contained combat element of the CPKF.[29]

While the CPKF saw no combat, it was tasked with guarding prisoners, particularly those of the Grenadian People's Revolutionary Army, and with other military police functions. The Jamaica Defence Force personnel were much appreciated by their United States military counterparts and the strong sense of military professionalism enabled the JDF contingent to perform well and extricate itself from Grenada with no blemishes upon its reputation despite the fraught internal situation following the American military intervention.[30] No major allegations of abuse were levelled at the JDF units.

As noted in the introductory chapter, the Jamaica Defence Force has a good relationship with the Regional Security System and has operated in coordination with the latter on many regional operations, usually in support of humanitarian assistance and disaster relief. In addition, and again as detailed in the introductory chapter, the JDF was prepared to commit a full rifle company to Trinidad in 1990.

However, these experiences, and JCF support operations during periods of unrest, did not prepare the JDF for its most intense operation to date – in 2010, against Jamaica's criminal gangs.

The Tivoli Incursion 2010

The Tivoli Incursion was an operation launched by the JCF and the JDF to secure the notorious drug lord Christopher 'Dudus' Coke who led the infamous Shower Posse drug cartel in Kingston. The operation lasted a full month – from 23 May 2010 to 23 June 2010 – and saw the JCF and the JDF engaged in urban combat with armed criminal gang members. The situation was complicated by an apparent link between the then Jamaican Prime Minister, Bruce Golding, and Christopher Coke. The vast majority of the fighting in Tivoli Gardens took place between 24 May 2010 and 25 May 2010, though sporadic actions took place thereafter as the JCF and the JDF sought to find Coke and detain him pending extradition.

This was further complicated by the decision by the United States government to request the extradition of Coke in 2009, thus setting in motion a sequence of events that would culminate in the efforts of the JDF and the JCF to secure Coke and to extradite him to the United States. The confrontation that followed would cost at least 73 civilian lives, with four members of the security forces also being killed in action, several vehicles being destroyed and over 500 people arrested. It also involved the use of mortars on urban areas by the JDF as well as the extensive use of armoured vehicles by both the JDF and the JCF, with one of the JCF's armoured rescue vehicles being seriously damaged during the fighting, having been briefly abandoned.

The early sequence of events, in respect to the request for extradition and the process of proceeding in that regard, was described as follows by the West Kingston Commission of Inquiry, noting the roles of the Commissioner of Police, the Chief of Defence Staff (CDS), the Prime Minister and the Attorney-General:

> 3.5. On 24 August 2009, then CoP Hardley Lewin telephoned CDS Stewart Saunders and told him that a request for the extradition of Coke was to be made by the USG to the GoJ.
>
> 3.6. CDS Saunders and CoP Lewin went to advise the Minister of National Security, Mr Dwight Nelson. Mr Nelson was briefed as to the information, which the Heads of the security forces had, and he advised them to report to Prime Minister Golding. Accordingly, they briefed the Prime Minister at his official residence the same afternoon. Mr Golding testified about the information he received. Under cross-examination by Mr Linton Gordon on 11 February 2015, he said –
>
> "I did not get the impression from Gen. Saunders or CoP Lewin that they were seeking a direction from me. The USG wanted to alert me and CoP Lewin told them that it was his responsibility to alert me… I was alerted by the Heads of the security forces that an extradition warrant for Christopher Coke would be arriving the following day… I spoke to the Attorney-General late that evening to tell her what the Heads had told me. Ultimately, it was her call to make."
>
> …
>
> 3.10. When the former Attorney-General, Ms. Dorothy Lightbourne, gave evidence, she said that Prime Minister Golding telephoned her on 24 August 2009 and told her that a request for Coke's extradition was on its way. The next day, she received a telephone call from the Office of the Director of Public Prosecutions (DPP). It was the Deputy DPP who said that there was someone from the military in her office and the

person wanted to discuss the extradition with Ms. Lightbourne. Ms. Lightbourne said "I would not entertain it since it had not come through the proper channels, that is to say, the procedure and protocol for dealing with an extradition request had not been followed".

3.11. The proper procedure as represented to us was, in summary –

(a) A request for extradition is made by the Requesting State to the Ministry of Foreign Affairs of GoJ;

(b) The Ministry of Foreign Affairs then sends the documentation to the Ministry of Justice. An administrative officer prepares a letter in standard form addressed to the DPP and sends the letter and the documents received from the Requesting State to the DPP;

(c) The DPP prepares a draft of the document known as an "Authority to Proceed" and forwards it to the Attorney-General, assuming that the GoJ is going to proceed with the extradition.

3.12. On the morning of 26 August 2009, Ms. Lightbourne received a Diplomatic Note containing the Request for Extradition and the several supporting documents duly authenticated. On the same day, an approved document "Authority to Proceed" was sent to her.[31]

This process, starting in 2009, left ample room for Coke to be alerted to the possibility of his extradition and given his evident political connections, the Commission of Inquiry believes that it is probable that Coke was aware of these developments.

The JDF Chief of Defence Staff – General Stewart Saunders – and the Commissioner of Police, Owen Ellington – drew up plans and a joint headquarters was established. However, as the Commission of Inquiry established, the two did not plan in concert, with the JDF making its own plans and conducting specialised training:

3.25. Although it was understood by the leadership of the security forces that the operation would be a joint enterprise between the JDF and JCF, each Force developed its own plan. The JDF developed "Operation Garden Parish". The plan of the JCF was "Operation Keywest" which was the subject of an Operational Order. Nevertheless, a joint planning team met regularly. DCP Hinds stated that the plan to arrest Coke was completed in January 2010. CDS Saunders said that the JDF began to prepare a plan for Coke's arrest in January 2010. He said –

"Since the operation was to be joint with the JCF, they were fully involved."

3.26. Lt. Col. Andrew Sewell who commanded the Second Battalion of the Jamaica Regiment (2JR) returned from Moneague where 2JR had been on training exercises. He said that he became involved in planning for the operation in February 2010.

3.27. Lt. Col. Jaimie Ogilvie was the commanding officer of the First Battalion of the Jamaica Regiment (1JR). From the last week of August 2009, he was engaged in planning the operation to capture Coke. His first plan was presented at the end of September 2009 and was accepted. Further refinement of the plan continued through to December 2009, at which time he briefed CDS Saunders, Lt. Col. Sewell and CoP Ellington. In his witness statement, Lt. Col. Ogilvie said at para.9:

"Shortly before the New Year, I attended a meeting at HQ, JDF which was jointly chaired by the Commissioner of Police and the Deputy Chief of Defence Staff and including senior officers of the JDF and JCF. No operational plans were discussed but the meeting focused on guidance given by the Chairmen concerning the planning, processes and conduct of any operation to apprehend Mr Coke."

3.28. Lt. Col. Ogilvie stated that among the issues discussed and the guidance given –

"were the need to ensure that Mr Coke's rights were not violated, the rights of citizens were to be protected and the operation should consist of three phases – planning and preparation, search and capture, and the return to normalcy, the importance of examining past operations in Western Kingston, the need for disciplined but overwhelming force and the importance of the security forces having a positive impact on communities."

3.29. Between March and May 2010, 1JR did contingency planning, training and rehearsals. Emphasis was placed on the CDS's instructions for Opening Fire, Human Rights awareness, citizens' rights and issues such as span of control, de-confliction of unit boundaries, identification of friendly forces and the interpretation of the Emergency Powers Regulations were discussed and resolved.[32]

With both regular battalions of the Jamaica Regiment preparing for operations, the JCF made its own plans and it is still unclear as to how the two forces planned to work in synergy and as events would unfold, neither the JDF nor the JCF anticipated the level of resistance that they would face. Indeed, in respect of joint planning, the Commission of Inquiry noted:

3.30. We found rather disconcerting the evidence of CDS Saunders and CoP Ellington that neither knew of the other's plans, namely, OPERATION KEYWEST and OPERATION GARDEN PARISH. We do not believe that these were matters for secrecy at the highest was joint as between the two forces, the respective plans should have been seen and discussed certainly at the level of the respective Heads.[33]

One observation that was not made by the Commission of Inquiry was the issue of joint training for the operation. The JDF and JCF cooperate on a regular basis but it seems that neither force believed that they would face coordinated resistance, though there was a good understanding of the types of weapons available to Coke.

Prior to the beginning of the operation to seize Coke, Prime Minister Golding addressed the nation on 17 May 2010, apologised for his efforts to lobby the United States and questioned the evidence gathered in support of the United States' request for extradition. Golding apparently took both the JDF and JCF by surprise when he said, in announcing support and authorisation for the extradition to proceed:

This matter of the extradition has consumed too much of our energies and attention and has led to a virtual paralysis that must be broken…The nation's business cannot continue to be disrupted and distracted by the ordeal of the last several months.[34]

Apparently neither General Saunders nor Commissioner Ellington were informed of the decision to sign the authorisation to proceed and, as such, were completely taken by surprise. This was to prove costly as the Shower Posse was able to plan and mobilise.

The reaction in Tivoli Gardens was manifested in overt displays of support for Coke. Barricades began to be erected at the entrances of the neighbourhood and the Shower Posse began to mobilise and arm itself with an eclectic array of rifles and handguns and openly display these as they mounted patrols along the barricades.

Simultaneously, Coke mobilised the civilians of the neighbourhood, with whom he had cultivated a 'Robin Hood' type image. This led to a series of demonstrations which served to focus attention on the area. In addition, Coke mobilised other Jamaican gangs who sent armed supporters – perhaps 300 in all – to reinforce the Shower Posse. As the Commission of Inquiry noted:

> 3.44. Some 600 women, mainly dressed in white, took to the streets of West Kingston on 20 May demonstrating against execution of the warrant on Coke and pledging their loyalty to him. Placards exemplified the esteem in which these women held Coke: "Without Dudus, there will be no Jamaica"; "Next to God, Dudus"; "Jesus die for us, we will die for Dudus".
>
> 3.45. On the same day, the barricading and fortification of Tivoli Gardens were accelerated. The entrances to and the exits from the community were blocked. We were shown a large number of films and photographs of the blockading of Tivoli Gardens up to 23 May 2010. CoP Ellington's witness statement neatly encapsulates the nature of the barricading –
>
> "The barricades were constructed from old vehicles, old appliances, heavy equipment, scrap metal, sandbags and other solid materials. Several of the barricades had explosives embedded in them, with trigger mechanisms operable from inside residences. Road blocks were also mounted in other Corporate Area communities where gangs aligned to the Shower Posse had their bases."
>
> 3.46. We saw evidence of propane gas cylinders within the barricades and on a roadway. Barbed wire was used to block access to a street. Spanish Town Road was blockaded to prevent access to Tivoli Gardens. Near Darling Street, the access way to the community was heavily blocked. The sandbags referred to by CoP Ellington were used not only as blockade reinforcements but also as firing positions. The films and photographs, taken by the National Intelligence Bureau (NIB), captured images of men wearing bullet proof vests; men with night vision goggles; men piling sandbags; men with rifles and men keeping look out. Women were also seen watching the barricading in progress.
>
> 3.47. Fortification of Tivoli Gardens was swift and comprehensive. Intelligence available to the JCF and the JDF on a continuing basis was to the effect that, in the days leading up to 24 May, some 300 gunmen from all over Jamaica and loyal to Coke, had migrated into Tivoli Gardens and other parts of West Kingston. They had come to assist Coke and local gang members in resisting any attempt by the security forces to enter the Tivoli Gardens' community and arrest Coke.[35]

It was thus evident to both the JDF and JCF that they would face intense armed opposition from the Shower Posse and other gangs and that their foray into Tivoli Gardens would be fiercely resisted. The 1JR and 2JR (the first and second battalions of the Jamaica Regiment respectively) were assigned to support the JCF. 1JR was to establish a cordon around Tivoli Gardens, creating a buffer, while 2JR was assigned to actively support the JCF in apprehending Coke. Both battalions were fully mobilised and the remaining JDF V-150 armoured personnel carriers were assigned to support the respective battalions. In total, some 800 JDF personnel and 370 officers of the JCF were involved in the Tivoli Gardens incursion, with attendant support from other JDF and police units and with the full political backing of the government of the day. To date, Tivoli Gardens remains the JDF's biggest internal security operation.

The Tivoli Gardens gangs and their allies launched a series of attacks on the JCF with the aim of demoralising and/or deterring them from entering the neighbourhood. On 23 May 2010 alone, the following attacks were made:

5.30 a.m. Roadblocks mounted at the intersection of West Street and East Queen Street

7.58 a.m. Denham Town Police Station completely blocked in

8.04 a.m. Beckford Street and all roads leading to West Kingston blocked

6.30 a.m. Central units came under heavy gunfire while attempting to clear blockage

7.32 a.m. Industrial Terrace and Spanish Town road near Denham Town Primary School blocked

11.20 a.m. Darling Street Police report seeing men dressed in army fatigues, helmets and bullet proof vests in a blue building in Tivoli Gardens packing sandbags and placing large guns behind them

12.07 p.m. Police in Darling Street, Hannah Town and Denham Town Police Stations came under sustained gunfire

1.48 p.m. Police under heavy gunfire in Hannah Town, as reported by the rescue unit in the area. About 100 men were firing shots at the unit

1.58 p.m. Rescue 4 reports a police officer shot in Hannah Town and on his way to KPH

2.00 p.m. Hannah Town Police Station evacuated. Personnel and Government property removed

2.15 p.m. Police under heavy gunfire in West Street

2.59 p.m. The back of Hannah Town Police Station was on fire and the Fire Department was summoned

3.06 p.m. Report of armed men moving towards Trench Town Police Station

3.12 p.m. Police uniforms reported stolen from Hannah Town Police Station

3.18 p.m. Trench Town Police Station under heavy gunfire

3.22 p.m. Fletcher's Land Police Station under heavy gunfire

3.44 p.m. Rescue 4 under heavy gunfire at the intersection of Regent Street and Darling Street

4.13 p.m. Men seen on top of Flying Squad building with guns

4.13 p.m. Duke Street and North Street blocked

4.23 p.m. Denham Town Police Station bombe

4.35 p.m. Denham town Police Station under heavy gunfire and the police calling for help

5.47 p.m. SAC unit under gunfire at Slipe Pen Road; advised to retreat

6.10 p.m. Police advised to abandon their vehicle on Slipe Pen Road. It is taken over by criminals

6.52 p.m. and 7.36 p.m. Reports of attacks being planned for Vineyard Town Police Station and Central Village Police Station respectively

8.49 p.m. Maxfield Avenue and Spanish Town police under fire

8.54 p.m. Police under heavy gunfire at Sunrise Crescent near Red Hills Road

9.04 p.m. Fletcher's Land Police Station under heavy gunfire. Assistance sent

9.08 p.m. Report received that at 12.47 p.m. gunmen had invaded the Victoria Jubilee Hospital

9.12 p.m. A police vehicle crashed near that hospital. It is believed that the vehicle SAC 91 was stolen by criminals after it had been abandoned by its police occupants

9.50 p.m. Police attempt to clear road block at Flat Bridge and come under fire

11.37 p.m. PC Johnson's private vehicle was shot up in Perkins Boulevard

11.43 p.m. Police Officers in MPD 03 shot near Nannyville and the National Stadium

11.50 p.m. Police Corporal shot[36]

The JCF's Mobile Reserve, heavily armed and supplied with a number of armoured vehicles, was led at the time by Assistant Commissioner of Police Leon Rose. He led a team of 35 officers, with an APC in support to try to clear the barricades and regain control. However, in his own words:

> I saw a number of blockages of major streets – West Street; West Queen Street; Water Lane. On Industrial Terrace there was a barrage of gunfire coming from Tivoli Gardens and the Denham Town area near the Primary School. It sounded as though rifles were being fired. They were directed towards us, that is to say, towards Marcus Garvey Drive and Industrial Terrace. There was also gunfire from the vicinity of May Pen Cemetery. We had to turn back from Industrial Terrace. We could not clear the barricades. We had Intelligence that some of the barricades were booby-trapped. I heard on my radio that the team that was on its way to Denham Town police station could not proceed because of the intensity of the gunfire. The Commissioner and I were going from a different location than the team. They went from Spanish Town Road whereas we approached from Industrial Terrace. This was about 10.30 a.m.[37]

An APC at Hannah Town Police Station was severely damaged and had to be abandoned. Several police detachments were ambushed, leading to many casualties among the JCF personnel, with Constable Jason Davis being killed at 5:46 a.m. on 24 May 2010 and several JCF vehicles being destroyed or damaged.[38] The JDF was not immune from these attacks with their Up Park Camp being attacked on 23 May 2010 though the gunfire was described by Lieutenant Colonel David Cummings as being 'ineffective'.

The JCF and the JDF, after facing this onslaught, decided that they needed to take decisive action and at 8:00 a.m. on 24 May, the JDF soldiers of 1JR and 2JR and police officers, including members from the Mobile Reserve were assembled for briefings at Up Park Camp and Harmon Barracks, by their respective unit commanders. These briefings included detailed instructions on the use of force and the need to respect the human rights of the people in Tivoli Gardens. In addition, the commanders tried to lay down clear rules of engagement for the impending operation.[39]

Both JDF units – 1JR and 2JR – along with the JCF faced intense resistance as they moved by platoons into Tivoli Gardens. Captain Garth Anderson of 2JR stated:

> No.6 platoon encountered heavy resistance from gunmen located in the Coronation Market, inside the MPM building and on high-rise buildings located to the north of Tivoli Gardens in the vicinity of Tivoli Court. The gunmen were engaged with aimed controlled fire by members of the platoon. It is believed that these gunmen fled north towards the Denham Town community.[40]

The task of finding Coke and transporting him to a pre-determined location was assigned to Major Mahatma Williams and the Combat Support Battalion (CSB). His APCs (V-150s) and front end loader engineering vehicles were also tasked with clearing barricades. The CSB was also faced with sustained resistance and while its personnel were much better protected than those of 1JR and 2JR, they made extremely slow progress and the intensity and ability of their opposition surprised them. Major Williams deposed as follows:

> 30. There were multiple roadblocks; the first being at the railway crossing on Industrial Terrace. As the unit slowed down to allow the front end loader and APCs to clear the first blockage, a coordinated barrage of gunfire as per an ambush came from the Tivoli Gardens buildings off to our northeast and the open lot to the east.
>
> 31. Harassing gunfire was also coming from the direction of Universal Freight Handlers.
>
> 32. Overall, the bullets were mainly hitting the asphalt and a low wall to the east of us. Trees in the open lot were also being hit. The sandbags on the vehicles were hit and as a result their contents emptied out.
>
> 33. The firing from Universal Freight Handlers disrupted the movement of the support elements of the unit but was not significant enough to warrant being cleared. Up to this point my unit had suffered no casualties except for a few people who were suffering from heat related injuries.

34. The gunmen who had occupied Tivoli Gardens did not get the opportunity to detonate any explosives in the barriers where my unit manoeuvred.[41]

If this was not bad enough, the JDF received intelligence that one .50-inch anti-materiel rifle was available to the armed gangs in Tivoli Gardens. These weapons would have easily penetrated the lightly armoured V-150s of the JDF and the APCs of the JCF Mobile Reserve, not to mention the soft-skinned cars, jeeps and trucks of the security forces. Major Williams described the steps taken to protect the unarmoured JDF vehicles to the Commission of Inquiry, showing a commendable display of innovation and initiative:

18. We reinforced our patrol vehicles with sandbags strapped to the bonnets and dashboards so that the drivers had some degree of cover and also to protect the engines and radiators.

19. Our patrol vehicles were further fortified with bullet traps to make a barrier between the driver/commander in the front and the tail-end gunner. This was done to ensure that, if the driver were shot, the persons in the back of the vehicle would be able to continue fighting.[42]

Bravo Company of 1JR, under the command of Major Kevron Henry found itself facing intense resistance at Coronation Market, in the vicinity of the destroyed Darling Street police station. He found that the resistance was organised, determined and quite effective. Major Henry estimated that his unit took three hours to advance 500 metres, facing gunfire at every step of the way, with the resistance being extremely well coordinated.

Bravo Company's No.4 Platoon came under such heavy resistance that, at Foxy's Plaza, they took sufficiently heavy casualties that they were compelled to withdraw to prevent their own positions from being overrun. As the Commission of Inquiry noted:

4.82. The casualties suffered by No.4 platoon greatly retarded its progress and prevented the soldiers from securing the high ground of Foxy's Plaza which was critical to domination of the area. Maj. Henry told us that "securing the high ground of Foxy's Plaza would give the security forces watch over surrounding areas and various avenues of approach". It was imperative that this objective be achieved because the gunmen had forced the security forces along certain corridors and were manoeuvring in an orchestrated and preplanned manner "so as to create effective lanes and draw the security forces into kill zones."[43]

This impasse continued until 2nd Lieutenant D. Trowers used a V-150 APC to seize the nearby PassaPassa Plaza. The use of the V-150 provided sufficient protection to the troops to regain the initiative. Bravo Company gradually moved forward through the area and secured Foxy Plaza, PassaPassa Plaza and other key areas in the Coronation Market area. However, throughout the night of 24 May and into the early morning of 25 May, Bravo Company reported very intense gunfire with all section commanders reporting such incidents with attendant casualties. The JDF was faced with at least one .50-inch calibre Grizzly sniper rifle which, alongside rifle-calibre weapons, proved to be a major obstacle to their operations. The CSB was forced to deploy teams also equipped with .50-inch calibre sniper rifles to neutralise these opponents. The JCF did likewise but their rather more indiscriminate use of these weapons was not particularly useful.

Sporadic resistance continued all day of 25 May but the gunfire grew progressively less as the day went on. By 6:00 p.m. on 25 May, Bravo Company was finally able to secure the Denam Town area and, with the support of the JCF Mobile Reserve, was able to establish complete domination of the area. The 48 hours of fighting amply demonstrated the challenge that the JDF and JCF faced in dealing with the Tivoli Gardens gangs and was an ominous portent for future operations. The level of resistance encountered is partly reflected in the fact that some 115 weapons and over 15,000 rounds of ammunition were seized during the course of the operation, with only a fraction of the possible arsenal of the gang members being seized.

Over the next few days, the JDF and JCF found themselves having to clear out pockets of resistance. One of the more controversial aspects of the JDF's involvement was the decision to use 81mm mortars in urban terrain, the use of the said weapons being directly ordered by Chief of Defence Staff Saunders who explained his logic as follows:

There was a need to keep women and children behind doors. Experience had shown that they were used as human shields. I needed the troops to have as much access as possible and to create a different sound in the operational area. They were fired under observed and controlled conditions. Each target was pre-determined and they were fired into three open areas. They had the desired effect. They created some disorientation and we never suffered many injuries and fatalities. There is no record of women and children killed during the operation. The mortars caused persons to remain behind doors.[44]

The mortars fired 37 rounds at three designated areas – the Seprod field, an open area near to the Community Centre in Tivoli Gardens and the football field on the eastern side of Tivoli Gardens – on 24 May 2010 and were under the command of Major Warrenton Dixon who was responsible for controlling the mortars and observing their impact. It has been suggested that alongside terrifying the civilians at Tivoli Gardens, two civilians were killed by the JDF's 81mm mortars.

The use of 81mm mortars was to prove extremely controversial and their use came in for scathing criticism, both at the time of the event and during a subsequent Commission of Inquiry which raised serious questions as to the judgement exercised by the CDS in authorising their use and the observation and controlling of the weapons by Major Dixon. The Commission stated:

10.175. Although we accept that two open playing fields were targeted for landing the mortars, we condemn the decision to explode mortars inside Tivoli Gardens itself. The area chosen was a heavily populated built-up area which carried a great risk of injury or death to residents. Our reading of materials provided by INDECOM on the use of mortars in international humanitarian law (IHL), convinces us that the weight of contemporary opinion, policy and law is against the use of mortars in densely populated areas, such as Tivoli Gardens. In the circumstances, we endorse the characterization by Maj. Cobb-Smith of the use of mortars within Tivoli Gardens, as "irresponsible and reckless".

10.187. We adhere to our finding that, notwithstanding the unprecedented and vicious attacks planned and executed by Coke and his gunmen, it was reckless and irresponsible to fire mortars within the community of Tivoli Gardens in circumstances where, on Maj. Dixon's own evidence, the safety distances were not respected. Their use within the community was disproportionate. With respect to the concept of proportionality, we note that the Constitution as it then was in 2010 did not incorporate proportionality as a restriction on fundamental rights and, in particular, the right to life. As such, it is doubtful whether Counsel for the JDF can properly rely on that concept in defence of their use of mortars.[45]

After two days of heavy fighting, the JDF and JCF were able to overcome most of the armed resistance but could not locate Coke who had gone into hiding. Coke's capture became a major priority for the JDF and JCF who were understandably chastened from their experience in the heavy fighting that occurred. The JDF's intelligence network, combined with the JCF's network of informants was able to track Coke and thus enable an interception of his vehicle on 22 June 2010 at which point he was detained and subsequently extradited to the United States.[46]

This was a somewhat anti-climactic end to a traumatic internal security operation for the Jamaican security and political establishments. The JCF could not have achieved any of its objectives without the support of the JDF which itself began to discover its own shortcomings in respect of training and equipment in the face of heavy resistance from well-armed gangs. This would lead to a subsequent re-equipment programme and an expansion of the Jamaica Regiment to cater for internal contingencies.

Despite the fact that the Tivoli Gardens incursion was ultimately successful, it was extremely costly. At least 73 bodies were recovered from Tivoli Gardens and the dead included one member of the JDF and three from the JCF. Some 30 soldiers and 28 police personnel were also injured in the fighting. Civilian deaths are estimated at 69, including those of up to 26 gang members.[47] The scale of the fighting is illustrated by the fact that this death toll is significantly higher than that sustained in Trinidad's Islamist insurrection of 1990, reflecting the security challenge of armed gangs.

The Jamaica Defence Force Today

Of all the forces being covered in this book, only the JDF has an active military reform programme which involves a combination of expansion and reorganisation. As the JDF itself phrases its objectives in respect of expansion and reorganisation:

> Significant and evolving activities in the global security environment have led to an increase in the size and commensurate structural reorganisation of the JDF. In that regard the Force is moving forward, in keeping with international doctrinal and military best practices and strategic analysis; in order to revamp its joint strategic headquarters, overall command structure and to also expand and rationalise its domain focused line entities.
>
> This revamped structure sees the Force increasing in size from a North Atlantic Treaty Organisation (NATO) standard Reinforced Brigade (Rein Bde) structure to that of a NATO standard combined arms Division (Div) structure. This combined arms Div structure is achieved through the revamp of the Joint/Div headquarters and the creation of four Brigade formations in addition to the Regimental size Jamaica National Service Corps (JNSC).
>
> These four (Bde) formations; three Regular Force (The Jamaica Regiment (Jca Regt), the Maritime, Air and Cyber Command (MACC) and the Support Brigade (Sp Bde)) in addition to an expanded Jamaica National Reserve (JNR) will task organise existing units along with the proposed new units/entities to provide the necessary operational oversight and management of the Force's capabilities in the land, air, sea and cyber domains. This overarching structure facilitates a greater focus by the Chief of Defence Staff and the Joint staff on matters of strategic importance to the Force, nation and region at large.[48]

Again, unique among armed forces of the English-speaking Caribbean, Jamaica has given some level of attention to establishing viable reserve forces and a cyber command. However, on the more negative side, Jamaica has placed less emphasis on its Coast Guard which is still relatively small and under resourced compared to the Jamaica Regiment. The JDF's Air Wing operates a very modern rotary wing component but its fixed wing assets have been severely depleted. In this regard, the Jamaica Defence Force is demonstrating its internal security priorities as the Jamaica Regiment has been called out repeatedly to assist the often beleaguered Jamaica Constabulary Force in anti-crime operations which turn violent.

Land Forces

From its original force, and one which persisted for a very long time, of two regular and one reserve battalions, the JDF land forces are being expanded to a very considerable extent. This may have been partly due to the events of Tivoli Gardens in 2010, which, as has been shown, was a traumatic event in Jamaica's military history as well as its internal security calculations. The JDF land forces are in the throes of a significant expansion of both its active and reserve formations and is on the path to becoming close to a small division in personnel strength.

The Jamaica Regiment – the land forces component of the JDF – describes itself and its strength in the following terms:

> The Jamaica Regiment is the operationalization of a terrestrial and combat focused Regular Force formation with an overarching operational headquarters in command of five (5) battalions; the First, Second, Fourth and Fifth Battalions the Jamaica Regiment (1, 2, 4, 5 JR) and the Combat Support Battalion (Cbt Sp Bn).[49]

Table 14: JDF strength

	Strength
Active personnel	Approx. 4,000
Reserves	Approx. 1,500

The land component of the Jamaica Defence Force (JDF) is the Jamaica Regiment, which fields three regular infantry battalions with at least one more being created. These units have mostly light arms but also operate the support weapons in the JDF inventory. The JDF created Geographic Commands to allow its formations to cover a wider area of the country:

> The ever evolving and increasing security concerns that affects Jamaica overtime has led to a complete restructuring and rationalization of the Jamaica Defence Force (JDF) in an effort to optimise the use of resources. This optimisation includes the creation of three (3) Geographic Commands that will conduct infantry operation in those specific areas covering the entire Island.

Bushmaster APCs of the Jamaica Regiment on patrol. (JDF)

Bushmasters exiting their base. (JDF)

trafficking and violent crime has also increased in recent years, giving it an enhanced internal security profile. However, in this context, only police officers have legal powers of search and arrest.

Meanwhile, the Jamaica Regiment has limited conventional military capabilities but joint training exercises with a variety of foreign countries – mainly the US and UK – maintain a reasonable level of infantry skills.[52]

As has been discussed, the JR operated a significant force of V-150 APCs – the figure of 15 being most cited. However, the bulk of the army's LAV-150 commando armoured personnel carriers, which were acquired in the 1970s, were not roadworthy by the early 2000s and were in dire need of repair or replacement, with only three being operational in 2009.[53]

With this in mind, the JDF in late 2013 signed a contract with Thales Australia for 12 Bushmaster 4x4 protected mobility vehicles. The vehicles are troop carrier variants equipped with Thales' SOTAS M2 multimedia communications system, a Caterpillar 3126E diesel engine, ZF 6HP502 ECOMAT G2 automatic transmission, W&E Platt machine gun ring, and provisions for government furnished communications. Deliveries began in March 2015, when the first three vehicles were delivered. Another three vehicles were delivered in November, and deliveries were completed in January 2016. A five-year support package is included in the contract. The JDF was well pleased with the Bushmaster and in 2020 a contract for a further six vehicles was placed.

The creation of these Geographic Commands necessitates the need for a third Regular Force Infantry Battalion to support The First Battalion The Jamaica Regiment (1 JR) and The Second Battalion The Jamaica Regiment (2 JR). To satisfy this requirement the Defence Board, on 15 May 2018 gave approval for the establishment of The Fourth Battalion The Jamaica Regiment (4 JR).[50]

The Regular Force, which now includes the 5 JR, also has a Support and Services Battalion, a Combat Support Battalion – which has the Protected Mobility Vehicle Squadron with its Bushmaster APCs – and an Engineer Regiment. The primary role of the JDF is to defeat or deter violence threatening the nation state and its people. While this includes the defence of the country against terrorism and external aggression, in practice it mostly undertakes counter-narcotics and anti-crime operations which have often required the mobilisation of the National Reserve.[51]

Jamaica's army is designed to be multipurpose, being able to provide national defence as well as internal security, with many of its missions geared towards counter-narcotics. The deployment of the Jamaica Regiment alongside and supporting the police to curb drug

Table 15: Details of JDF Bushmaster APCs

Type	Role	In service	First delivery
Bushmaster	Tactical/light utility	12 and 6 on order	2015

The Bushmaster APCs are in service with the Protected Mobility Squadron of the Combat Support Battalion. This CSB is described as:

> The vision of the Combat Support Battalion (Cbt Sp Bn) is to provide for the JDF a composite operational unit, equipped with the dynamic requisite skills, knowledge and attitudes for deterring threats against Jamaica in all types and stages of operations.

Two Bushmaster of the Jamaica Regiment. (JDF)

V-150 armoured car of the Jamaica Regiment. (JDF)

> Through the exercise of mission command, the Cbt Sp Bn will exercise flexibility in its planning, supervision and execution of operations in support of the Jamaica Regiment, thereby allowing the combined security forces the ability to secure the Jamaican populace and their legitimate interests…
>
> The Combat Support Battalion is now the Chief of Defence Staff's operational flexibility and manoeuvre element, allowing for mechanized infantry support to be made available in any operational area across Jamaica. It is currently the home of the Protected Mobility Vehicle Squadron, made up of the Caribbean's first and currently only fleet of Bushmaster Thales vehicles. The mechanized infantry allows for the movement of troops under protection in order to render assistance of varied forms to light infantry and other military units. The Unit provides this capability to units deployed across the island, with particular focus currently on assisting the Jamaica Constabulary Force with the conduct of internal security operations.[54]

A less glamourous but more important modernisation programme was undertaken with infantry equipment, as L1A1 SLRs and British pattern web-gear and helmets were replaced with US-made M16 rifles, M249 SAWs and US pattern helmets, woodland camouflage and web-gear. This switch to US pattern equipment has been quite widespread and has also affected the Jamaica Constabulary Force which now is also largely American armed.

The Jamaica Regiment also maintains a substantial support brigade which is a Regular Force, as opposed to a National Reserve, formation that enables the provision of both combat support and service support functions. The Support Brigade is the operational headquarters for four units: the Support and Services Battalion (Sp and Svcs Bn), 1 Engineer Regiment JDF (1 Engr Regt (JDF)), the Health Services Corps (HSC) and the Corps of Military Police (CMP).[55] Of these, the Sp and Svcs Bn has a strength of 20 officers and 700 other ranks, arranged into eight companies.

The 1 Engineering Regiment JDF is a recently created formation and provides civil and military support:

> 1 Engineer Regiment (JDF) was formed in August 1991 and became fully operational on 01 April 1992. Prior to this all military and civil engineering tasks were carried out by two sub-units under command of the Support and Services Battalion: the JDF Construction Squadron and the JDF Engineer Unit. An increase in national demand for military engineers led Headquarters JDF to seek and obtain the approval of the Government to form the Engineer Regiment.[56]

The National Reserve

The JDF's National Reserve is officially described as:

> The Jamaica National Reserve (JNR) is a multi-domain focused reserve force formation that has been expanded to include a headquarters element in command of four (4) units; the Third, Sixth and Ninth Battalions the Jamaica Regiment (3, 6 and 9 JR (NR)) in addition to the Support Battalion (National Reserve) (Sp Bn (NR).[57]

In practice, the National Reserve is an infantry force with each battalion comprising six companies, with a small number of Regular Force personnel attached to each NR battalion.

The Maritime, Air and Cyber Command

Rather surprisingly, Jamaica has opted to group its Coast Guard and Air Wing into an umbrella unit called the Maritime, Air and Cyber Command (MACC). While the Cyber category is as yet nascent and now finding itself a role as a viable unit in the form of the Military Cyber Corps. The Air Wing of the JDF and the Coast Guard are small units compared to the Jamaica Regiment and it is perhaps in recognition of this that these two formations have been subsumed under the MACC. The MACC is officially described by the JDF website as follows:

> The Maritime, Air and Cyber Command (MACC) is a multi-domain focused Regular Force formation with an operational headquarters in command of six (6) units; the First and Second Districts Jamaica Defence Force Coast Guard (1st and 2nd Dist JDF CG), the Jamaica Defence Force Air Wing (JDF AW), the Military Intelligence Unit (MIU), the Special Activities Regiment (SPEAR) and the Military Cyber Corps (MCC).[58]

The MIU and SPEAR are two units without effective parallel within the Caribbean and possess capabilities commensurate with their functions within resource constraints.

Air Wing

Table 16: JDF Air Wing strength	
	Strength
Active personnel	200*
Reserves	15
* Sanctioned strength as of 2009 was 189.	

Jamaica's Defence Force (JDF) Air Wing is also undergoing modernisation with its helicopter fleet being extensively modernised with new, more modern, Bell helicopters while a limited recapitalisation of its fixed wing fleet is being undertaken as additional maritime patrol assets are being sought.

The JDF Air Wing has no conventional military capabilities and its capability to undertake even support missions is limited. The service's BN2 has been withdrawn from use and is a ground instruction platform, while the new DA40/42s are primarily training assets with a secondary surveillance role. The Bell 412 and the Bell 407s are the principal SAR assets. Given the size of the country's EEZ and the regional issues with drug trafficking, the fleet is insufficient to provide the required SAR and EEZ patrol requirements. Nevertheless, it is sufficient to provide minimum level SAR in the direct vicinity of the island.

The JDF Air Wing has been dependent until quite recently on outside agencies for the provision of training, although this is increasingly being undertaken within the country, following the creation of a small training establishment in 2006 with Canadian assistance. The establishment of training schools for both fixed and rotary wing units – the Diamond aircraft for the former and the Bell 206 for the latter – will stand the JDF Air Wing in good stead in the future. The JDF is therefore alone among the armed forces of the English-speaking Caribbean in that it is able to provide a comprehensive level ab initio training for its pilots. This is despite the fact that the JDF Air Wing has only a single fixed wing aircraft. Any expansion of the fixed wing assets of the JDF, therefore, will find the service in good shape to provide trained personnel for its requirements.

Rotary Wing Assets

The JDF Air Wing's Rotary Assets are in No.2 Flight of the force. This Flight is an all-Bell outfit at present as the JDF's Air Wing, as noted earlier, has a long and very productive relationship with Bell. There was a brief interlude when a force of Eurocopter AS.355s were procured in the 1990s but Jamaica was to return to the Bell family in the twenty-first century when it would operate no fewer than four variants of Bell helicopters. None of the JDF's helicopters are armed. However, their helicopters have been used extensively in internal security operations, with some legislative measures becoming necessary to allow JDF and JCF snipers to fire from the aircraft during operations in urban environments. As with much of the JDF inventory, the Air Wing went through serviceability crises in the early 2000s.

The JDF Air Wing currently operates a mixed fleet of Bell 206s, Bell 407s, Bell 412s and Bell 429s. The fleet now has but a single Bell 206, two 412s and three Bell 407s of variable operational serviceability. However, the JDF is intent on phasing out all its Bell 407s and 412s in favour of a modern, uniform fleet of nine Bell 429s.[59] Lieutenant Colonel Brian Lundy, of No.2 Flight stated:

> When we assessed our operations, we realized that with the 206, the 407, the 412, that was already three different platforms that we had to maintain and get parts for … But having looked at what we need to do for the country, we have now decided to maintain two types. The Bell 206 that we use for training, and the Bell 429 which we use for everything else.[60]

The nine JDF Bell 429s are built to civilian specifications, with no militarisation being undertaken. But, in recognition of their purpose, the aircraft are equipped to carry Goodrich hoists and, for surveillance operations, are also fitted with Trakka Systems TrakkaBeam searchlights and Wescam MX-10 Gen-IV cameras. For the deployment of special forces, the aircraft are also fitted with fast-roping and rappelling equipment. As with many helicopters in the Caribbean, for firefighting missions, a 260-gallon (1,000-litre) Bambi Bucket from SEI Industries can be slung under the aircraft.[61]

The JDF Bell 429s will be the best equipped helicopters in the Caribbean but their capacity is significantly lower than the Bell 412s that they will eventually replace. This is deemed to be an acceptable risk as Lieutenant Colonel Lundy indicated that the new technology of the aircraft will make the investment worthwhile: 'Transitioning from the 412 to the 429, we get a nice glass cockpit, so what we have now is top of the line'. He reserved particular praise for the aircraft's four-axis automatic flight control system (AFCS): 'The automation is fantastic. When we went to the drawing board to decide what we needed based on the amount of over-water work, we wanted to ensure that pilot workload was reduced. So, all of our aircraft will have the four-axis autopilot.'[62]

In addition, a force of six Bell 505s is replacing the Bell 206s. This would ensure a homogeneity in the fleet that would aid in its long-term sustainability and maintainability. This is assisted by the fact that the Bell 505 and the Bell 429 will have a certain degree of commonality. These aircraft will also be used to train pilots throughout the Caribbean while augmenting the Bell 429s for internal security operations and in support of both the JDF and the JCF. Bell's press release stated:

> With a speed of 125 knots (232 kilometers per hour) and useful load of 1,500 pounds (680 kilograms), the Bell 505 is Bell's newest five-seat aircraft designed for safety, efficiency and reliability

Beech King Air 350R of the JDF Air Wing. (JDF)

Table 17: Jamaica Defence Force Air Wing Current Assets

Platform family	Platform variant	Primary role (general)	Primary role (specific)	Estimated in service	First delivery date
Beech King Air	350 WR		Maritime Surveillance	1	2018
DA40 Diamond Star	DA40	Trainer	Basic	2	2006
DA42 Twin Star	DA42	Trainer	Basic	2	2009
Bell 412	Bell 412EP	Logistics	Utility	2*	1998
Bell 206			Training	1	
Bell 407	407	Surveillance	Utility	3**	2007
Bell 429		Surveillance and Logistics		7 with 2 on order	

* H-23 and H-25 are in service. H-23 was repaired after an 8-year gap.
** H-31 is damaged (since July 2007 and in storage). This leaves three in service – H-30, H-32 and H-33.

using advanced avionics technology. Its similarities with the Bell 429 platform allow for a smooth pilot transition as JDF begins training operations. With a Garmin G1000, the platform shares similar avionics with JDF's Fixed Wing Trainer aircraft and reduces pilot workload, enhancing the students' learning experience.[63]

The mix of Bell 429s, with their surveillance equipment, and the Bell 505s in support will give the JDF a good level of air support within the requirement of their internal security framework. The Bell 429s may also prove to be reasonably effective maritime patrol and Search and Rescue Assets but they cannot carry out long-range patrols and are not equipped to undertake anything more than limited surveillance and patrol missions. For such tasks, the JDF requires an adequate force of fixed wing assets and it is in this regard that the JDF Air Wing has fallen on hard times with its inventory now reduced to a handful of aircraft with one tasked with maritime surveillance and patrol.

Fixed Wing Assets

Aside from the two DA 40 Diamond Star and two DA 42 Twin Star ab initio flying trainers, and one Beech King Air 350, the JDF Air Wing is in dire need of fixed wing assets. While the Twin Star can carry three passengers, the JDF has not found replacements for nor has aggressively sought such replacement for its once considerable fleet of Cessna, De Havilland Canada, Rockwell Commander, Beech King Air and BN-2 Islander aircraft. The fact is that the JDF has no viable transport aircraft and can no longer move either troops or cargo by air beyond the ability of its helicopter fleet.

The JDF's sole viable and modern fixed wing asset is a single Beech King Air 350 WR obtained in 2018. This aircraft is equipped with intelligence, surveillance and reconnaissance (ISR) equipment.[64] There are suggestions that the JDF may be intent on acquiring a second as part of its efforts to build its maritime surveillance assets, which include the acquisition of four additional Damen patrol vessels.[65]

Jamaica Coast Guard

The Jamaican Coast Guard underwent a period of uncertainty and varying fortunes in the first decade of the 21st century. In the period 2004–2006, the Coast Guard fleet was rejuvenated with three Damen SPa 4207 patrol craft and two ageing patrol boats HMJS *Fort Charles* and HMJS *Paul Bogle* refitted by Damen. The rest of the fleet consisted of old US-made Dauntless-class patrol boats and a number of interceptor craft and *Boston Whaler* type vessels. By 2012, the fleet was composed of the assets shown in Table 18.

However, because the JDF failed to procure spares beyond the warranty period, compounded by the country's poor economic condition, the fleet soon fell into disrepair. HMJS *Fort Charles* was decommissioned in 2012 and the other vessels were almost completely unserviceable with HMJS *Paul Bogle* being decommissioned in 2020 after a prolonged period of inactivity.[66] The three Damen SPa 4207s were virtually inoperable by 2012 though they were nominally still in commission.

Table 18: Jamaica Coast Guard vessels			
Name of Ship	**Length**	**Builder**	**Delivery**
HMJS *Cornwall*	42.8m	Damen Group	2006
HMJS *Middlesex*	42.8m	Damen Group	2006
HMJS *Surrey*	42.8m	Damen Group	2007
HMJS *Fort Charles* (P 7)	35.3m	Swiftships	1974
HMJS *Paul Bogle* (P 8)	32.3m	Lantana Boatyard	1985
Source: Jamaica Defence Force Website			

Table 19: Jamaica Coast Guard personnel strength	
	Strength
Active personnel	340 (estimated based on 2010 figures)
Reserves	50

In 2015, however, Jamaica concluded a peculiar deal with Damen whereby its three Damen SPa 4207s would be decommissioned and returned to Damen in exchange for two new SPa 4207s that Damen had in stock. The decommissioning and return of the JDF vessels took place on 8 November 2016 and it was intended, after refurbishment, to offer them for resale.[67] The two replacement vessels were named (after their predecessors) HMJS *Cornwall* and HMJS *Middlesex* and after undergoing modification and outfitting were delivered to the JDF in 2016. It should be noted that these vessels have an austere equipment suite and lack advanced surveillance systems or weapons larger than machine guns. However, the SPa 4207 is a cost-effective solution to Jamaica's maritime patrol needs and, like many other countries in the Western Hemisphere, Jamaica has decided to continue using the type. The two vessels now form the primary assets of the Jamaican Coast Guard and provide the country's sole ability to patrol its maritime domain.

The Jamaica Coast Guard, therefore, after its expansion, had the personnel strength shown in Table 19.

The Jamaica Defence Force (JDF) Coast Guard is tasked with mainly coastal internal security and maritime law enforcement missions, in addition to maritime safety tasks (primarily search and rescue). The core of its fleet is formed around the two aforementioned two Damen Stan Patrol 4207 patrol craft.

The Jamaican Coast Guard's ability to wage conventional combat operations is non-existent, but it can operate at the lower end of the force spectrum. The Damen Stan Patrol 4207s gave the coast guard the ability to undertake and sustain extended operations throughout its Exclusive Economic Zone, something its smaller and older patrol craft could not provide. After 2016, the two new Damen Stan Patrol 4207s have not met the fate of their predecessors and have continued to function in service with a very high degree of serviceability and availability for missions.

Also of importance, the JDF Coast Guard's interceptor craft provide it with the ability to interdict go-fast vessels. That said, maintenance and spare parts are an ongoing problem, with a significant proportion of the small fleet out of operation at any one time. The capability was recently boosted through the donation of five Boston Whaler 37ft patrol vessels and five SAFE (secure all-around flotation equipped) boats, delivered over a number of years ending in 2019, as gifts from the United States.[68]

New Damen SPa 4207 vessel of the Jamaica Coast Guard. (Damen Shipyards)

FCS 5009-class *Nanny of the Maroons* of the Jamaica Coast Guard. (JDF)

HMJS *Cornwall* and HMJS *Middlesex*. (Damen Shipyards)

types which, together with the procurement of a supply of spare parts, should ensure their serviceability in the short to medium term.

The Jamaica Coast Guard participates in exercise Tradewinds, which is organised by US SOUTHCOM and which is a necessary tool to promote regional cooperation and provide training to Caribbean security forces to address drug trafficking, organised crime, human and weapons trafficking, and illegal fishing. However, the JDF Coast Guard is still one of the weaker ones in the region – being much smaller than either the Trinidad or Bahamas units. Of note, current plans call for the coast guard to grow its personnel strength to around 450.

Jamaica's older fleet of interceptors, however, is of varying serviceability and has not been without problems of maintenance and product support and it is questionable as to whether any of the older vessels are still in service. The close relationship the JDF Coast Guard maintains with the United States has enabled the Coast Guard to replace its force of interceptors that are of two principal

The Jamaica Defence Force (JDF) contracted Damen Shipyards Group to build two new Stan Patrol 4207 vessels to replace the core of the JDF Coast Guard's fleet, which consisted of three vessels of the same type. The old vessels were decommissioned in November 2016

Table 20: Jamaica Coast Guard Current Fleet

Class	Manufacturer	Role	In service	Commissioned
County (Damen Stan Patrol 4207)	Damen Shipyard	Patrol craft	2 and 2 on order	2017
Damen FCS 5009	Damen Shipyard	Patrol craft	1 and 1 on order	2020
Dauntless	SeaArk Marine	Patrol craft – inshore	4	1992 (doubtful serviceability)
Fast Coastal Interceptors	Silver Ships Theodore	Patrol craft – fast	3	2003 (doubtful serviceability)
Fast Coastal Interceptors	Nor-Tech	Patrol craft – fast	4	2008 (doubtful serviceability)
6m Fast Patrol Boat	Boston Whaler	Patrol craft – fast	1	2008 (doubtful serviceability)
9m Fast Patrol Boat	Boston Whaler	Patrol craft – fast	1	2008 (doubtful serviceability)
Justice	Boston Whaler	Patrol craft – fast	5	2015
SAFE International	Secure all-around flotation equipped	Patrol craft – fast	5	2015

Another view of the HMJS *Cornwall* and HMJS *Middlex*. (Damen Shipyards)

HMJS *Nanny of the Maroons* at sea. (Damen Shipyards)

and the new ones, HMJS *Cornwall* and HMJS *Middlesex*, entered service in March 2017.[69] The core responsibility of the patrol fleet will remain monitoring Jamaica's Exclusive Economic Zone, and cracking down on illegal fishing, drug trafficking and weapons smuggling.

Subsequently, the JDF Coast Guard moved to place further orders with Damen for two more SPa 4207 patrol boats and two FCS 5009 vessels.[70] One of the latter vessels, now named *Nanny of the Maroons* has been commissioned.[71] Jamaica has, like many other Caribbean countries, chosen to place its trust in Damen vessels but has not opted to equip them with advanced equipment but has rather chosen to follow a path of cost-effectiveness and limited though adequate weaponry for the constabulary role.

Jamaica has also invested – like Trinidad and Barbados – in a comprehensive coastal radar network. However, unlike the latter two countries, Jamaica has not opted for an Elta system but rather for a network based around the Thales Coast Watcher radar. Under a US$ 100 million contract, Jamaica Defence Force (JDF) will be provided with a turnkey system that centres around a series of Coast Watcher 100 radars, electro-optical sensors, and Global Maritime Distress and Safety System (GMDSS) radios. These will be integrated with a National Control Centre to provide data fusion from these sensors.[72]

In 2019, the Jamaica Coast Guard was divided into two districts – the 1st District and the 2nd District. At present, the 1st District possesses most of the fleet's holding but it is expected that when the remaining Damen vessels are delivered, the 2nd District will receive a full inventory of viable patrol assets.

Conclusion

Compared to the defence forces of Trinidad and Tobago and the Commonwealth of the Bahamas, the JDF confronts similar security threats in the maritime sphere and from narcotics trafficking. Like Trinidad, it also faces a difficult internal security environment with its forces being deployed to augment a beleaguered police force against well-armed organised gangs. However, the JDF faces these challenges with the spectre of having to rely on a weak Jamaican economy to support its requirements. To the credit of the JDF and Jamaica, decisions have been made and resources allocated to keep the force viable in the years to come. Nonetheless, this viability will be contingent on adequate budgetary support being made available for the maintenance and upkeep of JDF assets and it remains to be seen if this will be forthcoming in the future.

6
TRINIDAD AND TOBAGO DEFENCE FORCE

The Trinidad and Tobago Defence Force (TTDF) is perhaps the most experienced unit in the English-speaking Caribbean. In 1990, it successfully quelled an Islamist insurrection which held the then government hostage. Prior to that, it suffered the ignominy of a mutiny in 1970. Today, despite being one of the larger forces in the region, it is suffering from a severe crisis of asset availability with an attendant dramatic decline in combat efficacy. The TTDF, however, has been increasingly seen as an asset to support the beleaguered police service in a battle against criminal gangs and while its deployment is quite heavy, investment in enhancing its capabilities is very limited.

Trinidad and Tobago

Trinidad and Tobago lies at the southernmost point of the Caribbean Archipelago, only 11km off the coast of north-east Venezuela. Trinidad and Tobago is an industrialised society with a high literacy rate and large petrochemical, petroleum and natural gas sectors. Literacy exceeds 98 percent and education up to tertiary level is free.[1] While there is income disparity and some level of deprivation, Trinidad's per capita income is no less than US$ 21,000 in nominal terms with a very high human development index.[2]

Demographically, the country has a stable population of just over 1.3 million, with 35.4 percent of the population being of

Indian origin, 34.2 percent of African descent and 22.8 percent of mixed parentage.[3] In terms of religion, 57 percent of the population identifies itself as Christian, 18 percent as Hindu and 13 percent as having no religion. Adherents to the Islamic faith comprise only 5 percent of the population.[4]

Security Challenges

The growth of the North American cocaine market in the 1980s was to see a total transformation of the narcotics landscape in the country. While cocaine addiction began to increase – young Afro-Trinidadians being among the worst affected[5] – the country itself became a major cocaine trans-shipment point for cocaine originating in South America for onward progression to the United States,[6] aided by border surveillance, corruption and judicial and bureaucratic inertia.

Trinidad thus found itself confronted with an increase in narcotics shipments through its territory and a major increase in the number of addicts emerging in the urban communities. In addition, with the cocaine trade came the first major inflow of illegal firearms into the country.[7] Hitherto, few weapons were smuggled in and even those were handguns for criminals. The cocaine trade brought with it a new level of arms smuggling, largely of handguns, once again, but increasingly a small trickle of rifles and shotguns began finding their way into the hands of criminal elements who began to display increasing brazenness.[8]

More recently, the nexus between Islamic extremism, terrorist groups and organised crime has emerged a major and as yet insurmountable challenge. In 2015, no fewer than 35 Trinidadians were identified as fighting for ISIS with other family members supporting them, actively bringing the total to 89.[9] By 2016, this figure may well have been an underestimate as figures discussed in Trinidad's Parliament placed the numbers at anywhere between 102 and a staggering 400.[10] Trinidadian police intelligence suggests that between 10 and 15 Trinidadians have been killed fighting for ISIS so far, although reliable information is difficult to obtain.[11]

Trinidadians became 'poster boys' for an ISIS recruiting video made in late 2015 which included their children.[12] Indeed, in the said video, one identifying himself as Abu Zayd al-Muhajir had brought his three children to Syria in the Ar-Raqqah province while another – Abu Khalid, a Christian convert – used the video to proclaim that Muslims in Trinidad were 'restricted'. This was echoed by Zayd al-Muhajir and yet another Trinidadian, Abu Abdullah, who went so far as to encourage Muslims in Trinidad to support ISIS and its ambition of creating an Islamic Caliphate with some limited success.

Trinidad is also plagued by an epidemic of violent crime where well-organised gangs vie for control of inner-city areas and the very lucrative narcotics trade enables them to procure large quantities of weapons. Many of these gangs, it is to be noted, who are affiliated with Islamic extremist groups, have secured control over whole swathes of Port of Spain, the capital city, and have begun to expand their zones of influence and control. With private armies nearly the size of infantry battalions, they have begun to exert their power further afield, targeting the populous urban and semi-urban communities. The police have been largely ineffective in controlling these gangs.

The Trinidad and Tobago Police Service (TTPS), on 13 February 2017, had a sanctioned strength of 7,884 full-time officers with an 'actual strength' at that date of 6,768, a 14 percent or 1,116 deficit, and should in theory be able to exert control and authority over gang-controlled territory. In addition, the TTPS has support in the form of the Special Reserve Police (SRP) which were supposed to be a reserve force but some 2,496 are employed on a full-time basis with only 652 being part-time. Furthermore, the TTPS is well-armed with assault rifles and submachine guns and is well-supplied with vehicles. However, the TTPS, despite being well paid, is plagued by incompetence, corruption, lethargy and extreme levels of inefficiency which has left a large proportion of its vehicles unserviceable. Compounding this is an ineffective shift system that ensures that only 23 percent of the total strength of the TTPS is available on any given day. This unfortunate combination of factors has ensured that whole swathes of territory fall under the sway of criminal gangs. Into this internal security mess, the TTDF has been asked to participate in many joint patrols.

The Organisational Set-up

Trinidad and Tobago does not have a separate Ministry of Defence. All security matters, plus the fire services and passport control and immigration, are handled by the Ministry of National Security. Control of this Ministry is vested in the Minister of National Security who, as a member of the country's cabinet, is responsible to the Prime Minister.

The Minister of National Security is usually not a subject matter specialist and relies heavily on the advice of the leaders of the country's protective services. This also extends to the bureaucracy that is responsible for the day-to-day affairs of the Ministry, responsible for allocations, releasing funds for repairs and stores, and to clearing procurement. In a practical sense, the Ministry is run by its bureaucrats with the Minister having no power to hold them accountable.

The Trinidad and Tobago Defence Force is operationally controlled by the Chief of Defence Staff who in turn reports to the Minister of National Security but is not under the latter's operational direction. This preserves a relatively apolitical nature of the military. However, the Chief of Defence Staff has very limited powers and has little practical control over force development or structure as the latter has to be subject to financial approvals as well as to conform to the political wishes of the government of the day. This can prove to be a frustrating experience for any progressive thinking CDS.

The TTDF is under the control of the Minister of National Security who is in turn a member of the National Security Council. Directly under the Minister of National Security is the Defence Council and the Chief of Defence Staff in turn is nominally subordinate to the Defence Council.[13] In reality the Defence Council rarely functions and then only for a limited number of issues leaving the CDS to report to the Minister of National Security as needed and where necessary to the Prime Minister through the National Security Council.

It should be noted that while the CDS does have considerable administrative authority, its practical powers are limited to matters of force administration with very limited financial powers. The CDS has little to no input into overall national security policy which is largely the purview of the Minster of National Security under the direction of the Prime Minister. This means that while the CDS is consulted on major issues, his input is not usually decisive and not necessarily taken into full account in the development of policies.

The Trinidad and Tobago Police Service was and is a much more visible entity as might be expected and is under the administrative and operational control of the Commissioner of Police. The Commissioner of Police is probably the single most powerful yet most difficult post in the national security structure as the Commissioner is held responsible, by the public and by politicians for every increase in crime or criminality and also has to grapple with a dysfunctional procurement system which precludes timely replacement or repairs to existing systems leading to a very low level of operational efficiency and poor efficacy.

The Trinidad and Tobago Defence Force

The Trinidad and Tobago Defence Force (TTDF) was formed in 1962 prior to the country's gaining of independence from the United Kingdom. The TTDF, as established, had a land-based element – the Trinidad and Tobago Regiment (TTR), and a naval element – the Trinidad and Tobago Coast Guard (TTCG). A small reserve force called the Volunteer Defence Force (VDF) was also established.

The TTR was established as a battalion sized outfit while the TTCG was established with a modest personnel strength but with two capable patrol boats.

A BRIEF HISTORY OF THE TTDF

The Federation Experiment

The Trinidad and Tobago Defence Force emerged out of an unsuccessful, but ambitious plan, to create a military force encompassing the whole English-speaking Caribbean, as described in the chapter on Jamaica. The failure of the Federation meant that local military forces needed to be established by the individual countries.

For Trinidad and Jamaica, with the dates for their declarations of independence set for August 1962, the need became acute as it became necessary to break up the existing, albeit very small, units of the West India Regiment. This enabled the formation of the defence forces of Jamaica, Barbados and Trinidad.

The Birth of the TTDF

Unlike Jamaica, and to a large extent Barbados, which had a long established and proud military tradition, and one which was maintained assiduously even after the end of the Second World War, the Trinidad Regiment had been disbanded in 1947 and its colours stored in Trinity Cathedral, Port of Spain.[14] The men of the Trinidad Regiment, by 1962, had aged considerably and were not fit for re-engagement in a military force, even if they had wanted to, as many had gone on into the civil service and the professions with considerable success and corresponding financial reward.

A new Trinidad and Tobago Regiment had to be forged and to this end Major, later Lieutenant Colonel, Peter Pearce-Gould, was to oversee the recruitment of officer cadets for the new military force. He recruited, among others, Major Stewart Hylton-Edwards who was to rise to become a company commander in the new TTR, and selected one Major Joffre Serrette, a Trinidadian who had served in the part-time Trinidad Volunteers before rising to the rank of staff-sergeant before being commissioned. Serrette had no operational experience and had only held administrative positions but was being groomed to become the Trinidadian commanding officer.

It should be noted that when the Trinidadian Minister of Home Affairs, Dr Patrick Solomon, announced to the country's Prime Minister, Dr Eric Williams, that he had re-established the Trinidad and Tobago Regiment with some seconded officers and NCOs and others from the disbanded West India Regiment, the Prime Minister was taken aback stating that he had never asked for a regiment but wanted instead a 'National Guard'.[15] The plan for the regiment, such as it was, was to replace the police service's paramilitary functions, allowing the latter to become a largely unarmed civil force.

From the outset, realising that Trinidad would not be able to afford a large military force, the land element was to consist of a single infantry battalion with three rifle companies to which it was

Dingo armoured cars of the TTR. (TTR)

Shorland APCs of the TTR. (Photo by Author)

planned to add later three volunteer rifle companies as a reserve.[16] The force would be led by a lieutenant colonel who, for reasons of economy, would also be the commander of the entire TTDF. The TTDF would consist of a single infantry battalion and a coast guard with a modest force of patrol boats. There was no air element initially envisaged for the TTDF though the need for a modest liaison and patrol aircraft capability was appreciated and would eventually emerge prior to 1970.

The initial batch of officers was recruited from an eclectic mix of civil servants, teachers, businessmen and immigration officers, many of whom had no military experience.[17] This would later become a source of friction as a new generation of Sandhurst trained junior officers would emerge and question the competence of their less qualified superiors. Nevertheless, the TTDF was established successfully and was able to assume its duties as a ceremonial force and as a support for the police service as required. The TTDF was never envisaged as being capable of being a force capable of defending the country against a major adversary but it was expected to be capable of internal counter-insurgency and operations in support of the police against rioting workers or left-wing agitations.

Training and Composition

As noted, there was considerable difficulty in recruiting qualified officers. This was gradually ameliorated as more and more Trinidadian cadets were sent to officer training academies overseas. A rather more serious problem was the lack of an officer 'caste' and a problem with the non-commissioned officers being unwilling to take responsibility for the often harsh and uncompromising, but scrupulously fair discipline that must perforce be part of any military force. These issues were particularly noticeable in the early years of the TTDF's existence but were gradually resolved as more and more trained officers and NCOs were able to assume responsibilities.

Training for the TTDF was largely done locally for other ranks but officers of the TTR were trained for one year at the RMA Sandhurst while officers for the TTCG were trained at the BRNC Dartmouth. There were also extensive training courses conducted in or by the United States and while there were some lacunae in operational training, overall the standard of basic training and the quality of personnel was quite high and professionalism carefully inculcated in the officer corps and other ranks.

The TTR in particular has always had a somewhat problematic conceptual role in the defence structure of the country. While the TTCG had a very clear maritime responsibility and embarked upon an equipment acquisition process that was well suited to its intended role and function, emerging as a very capable maritime unit with an enviable regional reputation, the TTR had no clear role. The TTPS still clung to its paramilitary trappings and in the absence of internal unrest beyond the ability of the police to handle, there was little call upon the TTR in respect of aggressive internal security duties. However, the TTR's training focused heavily on internal security with industrial unrest looming as a potential challenge in the late 1960s and early 1970s with training in crowd dispersal and control of industrial facilities being emphasised at some length with exercises including the occupation of such facilities against strikers.

One aspect that was heartening was the fact that the officer corps of the TTDF took its responsibilities as being loyal to the constitution very seriously. Despite a mutiny in 1970, occasioned in large part, as detailed below, by conditions within the regiment, the TTDF viewed itself as apolitical.

The TTDF, prior to 1990, saw no combat but in 1970, during political upheavals associated with the Black Power Revolution, elements of the TTR mutinied, led by Lieutenants Raffique Shah and Rex LaSalle. This mutiny while politically alarming, lacked any clear objective and ended in a tame surrender by the mutineers and later their acquittal by a court martial. The TTCG, in contrast, remained completely loyal during 1970 and some tension between the formation has existed ever since.

The 1970 Mutiny

The bizarre events of 1970 have been given all manner of political spin by people who were participants in the event and some officers either currently serving or now retired from the TTDF. Several intelligence reports on the 1970 mutiny indicated that there was political involvement in the events at Teteron Barracks, set against a tense political environment where the TTDF found itself witnessing a debate between a revivalist Afro-Trinidadian identity and a military still rooted in a colonial past.

Roots of Discontent

Lieutenant Colonel Joffre Serrette had taken over command in 1964. His subordinates were a motley crew of former civil servants, teachers and associated personnel with minimal military training and even less command experience. There were exceptions to this rule but many junior officers saw their seniors as uniformed popinjays with more interest in the cut of their uniforms and their perks.

In contrast, a new generation of officers, trained at Sandhurst and Mons were trying to turn the TTR into some sort of fighting force, though this might have been an exaggeration since resource and manpower constraints meant that at best the TTR could develop relatively limited

Messerschmitt-Bölkow-Böhm MBB Bo.105 CBS-4 – used for police support by NHSL before its loss. (Photo by Author)

combat capabilities. It was and is incapable of defending the country against a major external invasion as the correlation of forces and capabilities will always be against the TTDF.

There is, however, little doubt that with the arrival of these new officers, with a new outlook and new training, there was an increasing emphasis on training and readiness levels improved. The induction of a new generation of small arms and support equipment – the 7.62mm SLR, the first batch of which was received from Australia in 1966, replaced the .303 Rifle No.4 and the FN MAG GPMG replaced the Bren and Vickers guns, while the Carl Gustav recoilless rifle made its debut along with the 81mm mortar platoon and two Dingo armoured scout cars – helped solidify the feeling that the TTR was capable of being more than a mere ceremonial force and adjunct to the police service and was emerging, in its own right, as a viable entity.

There have been many theories, some ascribing political motives, as to the cause of the 1970 mutiny of the TTR. There is little doubt that the TTR was deeply concerned about the growing political and social unrest that characterised the street protests of 1970. It was also concerned about the increasing industrial and labour unrest supporting the Black Power movement and was inevitably concerned as to its role, should it have been called upon to aid the police in suppressing any protests. There was also the difference between the older officers, largely opposing the street protests, and the younger, radical idealists.

Yet another factor, however, was the lackadaisical approach to disciplinary matters within the TTR itself. This manifested itself in an inability of the senior ranks to deal even with insubordination on the part of junior officers towards seniors and a reluctance to enforce discipline. Major Hylton-Edwards recorded an instance of 2nd Lieutenant Lasalle raising his voice to the then CO TTR, Stanley Johnson, following a rowdy dinner in the Officers' Mess when five junior officers – led apparently by Lasalle and Shah – began banging cutlery and singing 'We Shall Overcome'. This lack of discipline stemmed from a leadership dispute.[18]

The real reason for tension in the TTR was directly related to a loss in confidence in the senior leadership. In 1968, Serrette had been arbitrarily relieved of his command by the government following rumours of a rift with the then Minister of Home Affairs, Gerard Montano, and replaced by Stanley Johnson, who was suddenly promoted to full Colonel in a remarkably short time.[19] This was not a popular decision among other officers and Stanley Johnson himself seems to have commanded little respect neither in regard to his ability nor his personality. In contrast, junior officers such as 2nd Lieutenants Raffique Shah and Rex LaSalle were quite charismatic and forceful leaders who also were politically aware of the developments going on in the country around them.

Other issues of a more prosaic nature, such as salaries (ordinary private soldiers then received between TT$ 24 and TT$ 36 a week, while lieutenants earned TT$ 336 a month) were major points of contention, though it has to be said, no arm of the government sector was particularly well paid at the time.[20]

Colonel Johnson came under severe criticism for being unable to address key issues in the TTR, namely a continuing shortage of manpower and deteriorating living conditions at the various barracks. The state of the regiment's fleet of vehicles was abysmal (something that would recur in 1990) and the combat effectiveness of the TTR was very debatable. Shah and LaSalle asserted that they tried to bring this to the attention of their superiors but this was to no avail. It was reported that on the eve of the revolt nearly one in six of the 600 personnel in the TTR were on sick-leave with some being deemed psychiatric cases.[21] This was a shocking level for a small force.

The Revolt

The TTR revolt was sparked in part at least by the decision of Prime Minister Williams to declare a State of Emergency on 21 April 1970. Led by Shah and LaSalle, some 150 soldiers mostly young – between the ages of 19 and 30 – were involved in the mutiny.[22] The takeover of the Teteron army barracks and the seizure of the ammunition bunker was conducted without any loss of life, with the only casualty being Major Henry Christopher who was wounded in his hand trying to wrestle a rifle way from Shah.

One of the two TTCG vessels – TTS *Trinity* – fired on the bunker with its 40mm Bofors gun from a range of 300m. This was remarkably close as the rebel soldiers had by this time armed themselves with rifles and GPMGs and had secured the six Carl Gustav 84mm rocket launchers held by the TTR. The Bofors fire was completely ineffective but it did give rise to a popular myth of their action having saved the day for Trinidad. Reality was somewhat more prosaic and less dramatic and the mutineers' failure to return fire saved the *Trinity*.[23]

The rebelling soldiers had amassed a substantial arsenal which included six Carl Gustav recoilless rifles, over 500 SLRs, several hundred submachine guns, 20 GPMGs, hundreds of Mills 36 grenades and well over 250,000 rounds of ammunition. In addition, they secured the five 81mm mortars of the mortar platoon.[24] There was no unit with this level of firepower available to stop the rebelling soldiers, the TTCG included.

In the capital Port of Spain, the Trinidad and Tobago Police Service (TTPS) was hastily armed with a bewildering array of small arms but mainly .303 Rifle No.4s and submachine guns. A few soldiers, many of whom were recent recruits and fresh out of training, were issued with SLRs and five rounds each as the country braced for a possible move by the mutineers from Teteron into the capital. The resistance that the TTPS and soldiers could mount was very limited at best and it is perhaps fortunate that it was not tested in any way with no lives lost.

The TTCG remained the most loyal military force available to the government with its 150 men and two patrol boats – TTS *Trinity* and TTS *Courland Bay* – being armed with 40mm Bofors. Its sole aircraft a Cessna 337 (9YA) piloted by Lieutenant Archibald overflew the rebel positions and tried to keep the government apprised of military movements and activity in the affected areas. Once again, the mutineers demonstrated remarkable restraint – perhaps indicative of their unclear motives – in that they did not fire on the aircraft, which, being unarmed, slow and low-flying, was vulnerable to ground fire from the mutineers' weapons.[25]

The TTCG, however, did arm its personnel with the infantry weapons it had available; SLRs and submachine guns were issued and landings practised from launches. With their additional armament of ship and land-based machine guns plus the undoubtedly effective 40mm Bofors L-60s aboard TTS *Trinidad* and TTS *Courland Bay*, the TTCG was the only military force that remained "loyal" to the government and, despite being very vulnerable to the mutineers' weapons, was prepared to confront and, if necessary, fire upon the mutineers.

A column of anywhere between 150 and 200 soldiers, armed with submachine guns, rifles, GPMGs and Carl Gustavs along with primed hand grenades was readied to move into Port of Spain. TTS *Trinity* chose once again to engage at a range of some 600m, well within the effective range of the Carl Gustavs' HE rounds.

The *Courland Bay* was still at TTCG HQ at Staubles Bay and had taken on board all shore personnel in case the facility needed to be evacuated. Some reports suggest that the *Trinity* was targeted by the weapons of the mutineers but they did not fire on the vessel though both sides knew the ship's clear vulnerability.[26]

In the course of the Trinity's shelling, one soldier, Private Clyde Bailey was wounded and had to be evacuated. Despite strong feelings that action should be taken, Shah and LaSalle, after abortive attempts to contact both the Trinity and the Cessna 337 9YA, and in spite of their overwhelming firepower, decided to withdraw back to Teteron to await developments.[27] In this sense, the lack of a clear agenda on the part of the mutineers was abundantly evident and as such whatever plans they may have had for moving into Port of Spain were not supported by any discernible political plans. The withdrawal to Teteron also saw the first steps towards de-escalation with Lieutenant Commander Mervyn Williams of the TTCG being sent as an intermediary given that he was widely respected and viewed very much as a paternal figure in both the TTR and the TTCG.[28]

The government of Prime Minister Eric Williams had been very reluctant to call for any external intervention during this crisis. However, he realised that his hastily and patchily armed police forces and few loyal soldiers could not resist a concerted push by the mutineers into Port of Spain, and given the reach of the Carl Gustavs and their undoubted efficacy against the TTCG's patrol boats, there must have been real concerns as to whether the Williams government could survive this crisis, though it is by no means certain that the toppling of the government was on the mutineers' political agenda.

During this confrontation, it was reported that a Venezuelan task force including at least two frigates had sortied towards Trinidad.[29] The vessels were intercepted by the TTCG and requested to return, which they did.

Despite holding Teteron for ten days, Shah and his colleagues agreed to talks and after Colonel Serrette was re-installed as CO – now promoted to Brigadier – issues such as the release of all political detainees and an amnesty for all participants in the mutiny were discussed. The mutineers gradually disarmed, initially by removing the firing pins from their heavy weapons – the Carl Gustavs in particular. Ninety men were charged with treason and mutiny, of whom 40 would be court-martialled. Several, including Shah and LaSalle, were sentenced to prison but, on appeal, the sentences were quashed and they were freed in 1972.[30]

Following the events of 1970, the TTR made strenuous efforts to reinvent and rehabilitate itself although it had to suffer the indignity of having its Carl Gustavs impounded by the police or sent to the Coast Guard for a number of years. The police service was emboldened by the temporary loss of face on the part of the TTR and sought to strengthen its paramilitary nature which it was able to do through the induction of many of the same small arms used by the TTDF and also by strengthening its Guard and Emergency Branch of heavily armed police officers.

The TTCG also played a role in rehabilitating the TTR with a deliberate effort to include parties of soldiers aboard naval vessels to enable them to participate in routine boarding operations as well as to introduce them to the maritime environment, and to build bonds between the formations which had been severely strained by the mutiny and the TTCG's role in attempting to suppress it. That being said, there was little animosity at most levels since a new generation of officers had replaced those tainted during the TTR mutiny and had moved on with improving the regiment's capabilities. These were to play a major role in the events of 1990.

Trinidad and Tobago's Day of Infamy[31]

Between the evening of 27 July 1990 and the afternoon of 1 August 1990, the Republic of Trinidad and Tobago suffered and overcame the second major challenge to its tradition of constitutional democracy since its independence from the United Kingdom in 1962. The citizens of the country witnessed the spectacle of the imposing figure of Imam Yasin Abu Bakr announcing the 'overthrow' of the government of Prime Minister Arthur N.R. Robinson.

While the death toll of 24 was relatively modest, it was a colossal shock to Trinidad's national psyche. The property damage and the consequent damage to the economy was severe and the country took a considerable period of time to achieve any degree of normality. However, the effects of the insurrection were not so much physical but rather the unleashing of hitherto underestimated ideologies of violent Islam. This was to have a major impact some 25 years later when the extent of Trinidadian involvement in ISIS became known.

The Trinidad and Tobago Regiment up to 1990

In 1990, the TTR was a small service, with two battalions constituting its entire strength. One of these battalions was a dedicated infantry formation while the other was designated the service support battalion and was responsible for all logistics and support elements including, it appears, a single mortar platoon of five 81mm mortars which, alongside some company level 60mm mortars, constituted the entire indirect fire support element of the TTR. The TTR also had a small force of Shorland armoured vehicles including at least three armoured cars and two armoured personnel carriers.[32] These vehicles, acquired in the 1980s, replaced the two Dingo armoured cars and were armed with smoke grenade dispensers and the armoured cars were frequently deployed with turret mounted GPMGs with the vehicle commander often carrying a B-300 rocket launcher as these became available in the mid to late 1980s. These vehicles were used for convoy escort and were deployed during the TTR's exercises in the 1980s.

The TTR was, in 1990, largely but not completely, re-equipped with Israeli Galil 5.56mm assault rifles which replaced the earlier L1A1 SLRs of British origin. The 7.62mm FN MAG GPMG was the standard automatic weapon for fire support, supplemented by a number of M60s from the United States and a small number of M2HB .5-inch heavy machine guns. Sterling and Uzi submachine guns were also in widespread use and were widely employed by radio operators with the latter being a particular favourite among the TTR's Special Forces. The re-equipment with 5.56mm weapons was far from complete in 1990 with perhaps only one-half of all personnel being re-equipped with Galils and with an average of only two Galils being available for every three infantrymen. The shortfall was made up by stocks of the old, reliable SLR which remained a very visible weapon among soldiers outside of the 1st Infantry Battalion and perhaps was even found among this formation.

It should be noted that the TTCG was still largely armed with the SLR and Sterling submachine gun but possessed two L-70 Bofors guns aboard CG-5 and CG-6 along with a 20mm weapon aboard CG-4 plus a plethora of heavy and medium machine guns aboard ship, making their deployable firepower not inconsiderable.[33]

Additionally, a number of Carl Gustav 84mm recoilless rifle systems remained ostensibly in service, having been purchased prior to 1970. These had been largely supplanted by Israeli B-300 systems – at least 13 of which were in service. The procurement of the B-300, as in the case of the Carl Gustav, was somewhat puzzling since the TTR did not envisage any encounter with a hostile force equipped with any type of armour. While the high-explosive rounds of the Carl Gustav were useful in demolishing buildings or hostile strongpoints, given that the TTR had not been trained to any extent in urban combat, the procurement of these weapons is one of the more curious acquisitions made by the TTR. However, during the 1990 insurrection, the B-300s were to come into their own with devastating effects both physical and psychological.

The 1st Infantry Battalion – led by Lieutenant Colonel Hugh Vidal – fielded some five rifle companies, designated 'A' to 'E, while the service support battalion – led by Lieutenant Colonel Carlton Alfonso – had two companies, an administrative company and a support company. The TTR had a total strength in 1990 of 1,513 personnel – 49 officers and 1,464 personnel below officer rank. For its modest size, the TTR was adequately equipped. A reserve force of approximately three rifle companies was available through the Volunteer Defence Force. The force was a well-balanced unit and possessed adequate firepower for its single infantry battalion.

The Trinidad and Tobago Coast Guard up to 1990

The TTCG began its operational history with two 103ft Vosper Ltd patrol boats –TTS *Trinity* (CG-1) and TTS *Courland Bay* (CG-2) – commissioned on 20 February 1965, each 31.4m long, displacing 123 tonnes and armed with L60 40mm guns. These were followed by TTS *Chaguaramas* (CG-3) and TTS *Buccoo Reef* (CG-4), commissioned on 18 March 1972, each 31.5m long and displacing 125 tonnes, being armed with Oerlikon 20mm guns. CG-1 and CG-2 were decommissioned in 1986 and CG-3 and CG-4 in 1992.[34]

These Vospers were followed on 15 June 1980 by two modified Spica-class vessels – TTS *Barracuda* (CG-5) and TTS *Cascadura* (CG-6) – each 40.6m long and displacing 210 tonnes. These vessels were equipped with L70 40mm guns plus Oerlikon 20mm weapons. These vessels were very advanced for their time and were well-liked locally.

Following a failed attempt at local repair and refurbishment in the late 1990s, these vessels were removed from service after nearly 15 years of inactivity. CG-5 was scrapped. While CG-6 remained ostensibly on the fleet list in 2019, at Chaguaramas Heliport, it was completely derelict, bereft of sensors, engines, weapons and accommodation. In 1990 both CG-5 and CG-6 were suffering from spares shortages and in dire need of overhaul.[35] These overhauls never took place and the vessels never achieved their full operational status, with their subsequent withdrawal from operational service and undignified fate epitomising the lack of foresight post-1990. This was demonstrated in the failure to overhaul and refurbish assets which served the country extremely well and which had been purchased as part of a well thought out fleet expansion programme that stretched from 1965 to 1980.

On 27 August 1982, four Souter Wasp 17m-class (TTS *Plymouth* CG27, TTS *Caroni* CG28, TTS *Galeota* CG29, and TTS *Moruga* CG30) were commissioned. In addition, the Coast Guard was augmented in the mid to late 1980s with vessels from the disbanded Police Marine Branch – one Sword-class patrol craft (TTS *Matelot* CG 33) and two Wasp 20m-class (TTS *Kairi* CG31 and TTS *Moriah* CG 32). All of these vessels have now been decommissioned.[36]

The years 1986 to 1995 saw the decommissioning of almost all of the TTCG patrol assets and the de facto retirement of CG-5 and CG-6 for want of serviceability as well as the inability of the TTCG to undertake routine maintenance due to severe funding shortfalls. This left the formation incapable of performing its assigned tasks on any sort of credible basis. This period, not surprisingly, saw a significant increase in narcotics and illegal weapons being shipped through Trinidadian waters.

On 10 June 1989, all vessels belonging to the Police Marine Branch, the immigrations, prisons, fire services and the port authority, were handed over to the TTCG to be made operational. When the vessels were handed over, not one of the eight launches of the Police Marine Branch was operational. Within six weeks, all eight launches were restored to service and put into a patrol cycle.[37] This spoke highly of the ethos of the TTCG which was attempting to continue its work despite severe resource shortfalls. The induction of these vessels provided the TTCG with assets for routine patrols at a time when its resources were under severe strain for want of repairs and spare parts due to budgetary issues.

In 1990, the Trinidad and Tobago Coast Guard was in dire straits with vessels being short of spares, in need of dry docking, and crew training suffering for want of seagoing experience. While CG-3, CG-4, CG-5 and CG-6 were nominally in commission, evidence suggests that only CG-6 was fully operational at the time of the 1990 insurrection. CG-5 was down to one engine while the hull of CG-4 was in such poor shape restricting it to calm waters. Despite these shortcomings, the force of CG-4, CG-5 and CG-6 was still the most potent naval unit in the English-speaking Caribbean and was worthy of some respect.

CG-3 was in commission but not operational to any extent. These three vessels did sortie during the insurrection with hastily gathered crews and were supported by a motley mix of support vessels including some of the Souter Wasp boats named above. Personnel strength was approximately 550 inclusive of its small Air Wing and its commando unit, the Special Naval Unit (SNU).

Air Assets up to 1990

The TTDF has had a military aviation component since 1966 when the Air Wing of The Trinidad and Tobago Coast Guard was formed with a single Cessna 337 (serial TTDF-1) which served from 1966 to 1972 when it was replaced with a Cessna 402 Utiliner (serial 201).[38]

A brief flirtation with military helicopters began with the formation of the Rotary Wing Flight in 1973 with the first of four Aerospatiale SA-341 G/H Gazelles (serials 9Y-TFN, 9Y-TFO and 9Y-TGU) coming into service. However, by 1976, these were transferred to the Air Division of the Ministry of National Security which morphed into the National Helicopter Services Limited in 1990.[39] This entity performed helicopter operations in support of the Ministry of National Security but also performed civilian tasks and earned revenue by supporting the country's offshore oil installations. It was and remains a civilian entity with neither its pilots nor ground-crew being military or police personnel.

In service, the Gazelles were joined by Sikorsky S-76 helicopters from 1981 with three such helicopters being eventually delivered (9Y-TGW, 9Y-TGX and 9Y-TJW).[40] The S-76 in its various incarnations was to prove very popular in Trinidadian service and the type is still in service. It should be noted that although the NHSL helicopters were deployed in support of the TTDF during the insurrection of 1990, they remained painted in their highly visible civilian colours of orange and white which, while not as garish as their current bright red and black livery, rendered their aircraft somewhat conspicuous to anyone looking at them. The country lacked any dedicated military helicopter force and did not yet have an effective law enforcement air support doctrine.

Besides the addition of a single Cessna 310 in 1985 (serial 202), the Air Wing of the Coast Guard stagnated for decades with capabilities being severely limited and aircraft being procured second-hand rather than new. The acquisition of an old Cessna 172 in 1991 added little to the Air Wing's capabilities and it was withdrawn from service

Cessna 310 of the Trinidad and Tobago Coast Guard Air Wing. (Photo by Author)

Cessna 402 and Cessna 310 of the Trinidad and Tobago Coast Guard Air Wing. (Photo by Author)

Cessna 172 and C-26 of the Trinidad and Tobago Coast Guard Air Wing. (Photo by Author)

in 1994 but spent at least six years occupying space in the Air Wing's sole hangar propped on tyres. The Cessna 402 was withdrawn from service in 1998 but again remained in the hangar on supports for at least two years.

In 1990, therefore, the air assets available to the TTDF included two Cessnas – a 310 and a 402 – and the four helicopters of the NHSL. These assets were not extensively deployed largely because of a lack of need but the helicopters did fly several sorties in support of the TTR. The NHSL helicopters, in particular its S-76 fleet, were placed at the disposal of the TTDF's Special Forces contingents.

1990 – A Baptism of Fire

The Jamaat-al-Muslimeen mustered a fighting strength of some 114 men. These were led by Imam Yasin Abu Bakr, with Bilal Abdullah acting as his effective second in command. Both Bakr and Abdullah along with a few others had received varying levels of training in weapons handling and terrorist tactics in Libya with some emphasis being placed on the construction of car bombs and other improvised explosive devices.[41] The majority of their 'troops' were semi-trained youth with a smattering of older personnel and were largely of Afro-Trinidadian descent from urban areas in Trinidad. They were motivated but lacked a clear objective.

The origin of the Jamaat's weapons is most curious as, with their alleged Libyan connections, one might have expected at least some Soviet-bloc weapons to enter their arsenal. Rather, the Jamaat relied on an elaborate and highly effective smuggling network with purchases being made legitimately in the United States and then smuggled into Trinidad sandwiched between sheets of plywood. These were then cleared through customs thanks to Muslimeen supporters in the customs and excise division – one of whom was very well placed to deliver such services.[42] This network was outstandingly successful in allowing the Jamaat to build a large weapons stockpile.

Weapons available to the insurrectionists were almost exclusively civilian pattern semi-automatic weapons available commercially in the United States. There was a preponderance of Ruger Mini 14s and a few M1 carbines were noticed along with a number of pump action shotguns. There was a mix of handguns, both semi-automatic pistols and revolvers, and a number of grenades were captured when the final surrender took place. There were no support weapons of any kind and there was no evidence of the insurrections having been trained to the extent necessary to make effective use of their weapons in urban or open combat.

TTR soldiers on patrol in Port of Spain during the 1990 Muslimeen Insurrection. (Trinidad Express Newspapers)

In the aftermath of the insurrection an assessment of the arsenal available to the Jamaat conducted by US Special Agents Thomas J. Bailey and Adam R. Price revealed that of the 135 weapons used in the insurrection and which were subsequently surrendered, 105 were purchased by Jamaat agent Louis Haneef, a resident of Florida. These included 17 Mossberg 'Persuader' and 26 Winchester 12-gauge shotguns, 25 M1 Carbines plus several dozen Ruger Mini-14 rifles.[43] The use of commercial pattern weapons is particularly noteworthy as is the manner of acquisition.

The Muslimeen Strikes

The first target of the Jamaat-al-Muslimeen was on the headquarters of the TTPS located on Sackville Street, Port of Spain. At approximately 5:57 p.m. on Friday 27 July 1990, a young man of African descent was observed approaching the Sackville Street entrance of the TTPS HQ[44]. A police officer, Special Reserve Police Constable Solomon McLeod approached the young man and they engaged in a brief discussion, pointing to the nearby Sacred Heart Church. As the young man walked away, he fired eight rounds into SRP McLeod, plus one into the air.

The death of SRP McLeod, and the shot into the air, was the signal for the occupants of a green station wagon to drive the vehicle from around the corner of St Vincent Street, whereupon, four occupants alighted, and the vehicle was then driven over the corpse of SRP McLeod and into TTPS HQ whereupon it exploded.

While this was happening, an assault group of 36 Jamaat members moved towards the Parliament building, fully armed and meeting no resistance from any policemen on patrol. The Trinidad and Tobago Fire Service, which emerged as unheralded heroes of the insurrection, responded immediately to the blaze at TTPS HQ but were forced to withdraw after coming under heavy gunfire from the Jamaat, though no casualties were apparently incurred.[45] The proximity of TTPS HQ, the main Port of Spain Fire Station and the Red House Parliament building are particularly noteworthy. The distances allowed for the easy movement of the Jamaat insurrectionists.

Storming the Red House

The attack on the Red House, the seat of parliament, was the centrepiece of the Jamaat-al-Muslimeen's assault. It was a brilliantly conceived operation that succeeded by any metric. At about 5:45 p.m., Hon. Joseph Toney, a minister in the Prime Minister's office, was on his feet addressing the chamber and engaging in some of the usual crosstalk that engaged the Trinidad and Tobago Parliament, this time with Mr Trevor Sudama, of the newly formed United National Congress (UNC) and once Mr Toney's cabinet colleague. Mr Toney asked him 'Who is your leader?' At that point there was a lot of noise and gunshots and the chamber was stormed by an assault group of 36 Jamaat insurrectionists led by Bilal Abdullah, a close lieutenant of Imam Abu Bakr and one who was subsequently seen as the Jamaat's most capable leader during the insurrection.[46]

Initially, given their uniform-like garb, Mr Toney thought 'it was a military takeover'; however, since the gunmen were chanting 'Allahu Akbar', the members of parliament soon realised that the gunmen were Muslims, with the gradual realisation that they were members of the Jamaat-al-Muslimeen who singled out government ministers and overwhelmed the security detail.[47]

TTR personnel armed with SLRs using a civilian pick-upi in 1990. (Trinidad Express)

Several civilians were shot. At least two – Mervyn Teague and Lorraine Caballero – being killed as they tried to escape or panicked. Ms Caballero's death was particularly traumatic as she was shot in the stomach and left to bleed to death. In addition, one member of parliament, Leo Des Vignes was shot, perhaps because of his panicking during the invasion of the parliament chamber. He later died of his wounds. At the parliament building, the following deaths in various circumstances are known to have occurred:

ASP Roger George
Estate Constable Malcolm Basanta
George Francis
Arthur Guiseppi
Helen Lavia
Lorraine Caballero
Mervyn Teague[48]

Attack 3: Seizing Radio Trinidad and Trinidad and Tobago Television

The assault on Radio Trinidad was led by Jamal Shabaaz who indicated that his group of 12 men left Mucurapo in three cars with weapons being sent separately and housed in a vehicle near to Radio Trinidad, on Maraval Road. The assault began after 6:00 p.m. and resulted in a complete takeover of Radio Trinidad within a few minutes. Shabaaz announced that his intentions were not to harm any of the staff members of Radio Trinidad and indicated that if they cooperated all would be well. The assault group met no resistance of any kind as there was no security presence.[49] Emmett Hennessy, a radio host, escaped but was shot and injured. An employee, Pius Mason, was shot and severely injured apparently in error. This infuriated Bakr who was quite enraged when he heard of the incident and he took measures to ensure that the civilian employees at Radio Trinidad and TTT were protected over the subsequent days as the army tightened its cordon and contained the insurgents.

TTR B-300 operator in position during the insurrection of 1990. (Trinidad Express)

Attack on TTT

While Imam Yasin Abu Bakr was ostensibly in charge of the assault on TTT, the actual operation was led by one Kala Akii-Bua. Entry into TTT was as simple and as facile as that of Radio Trinidad with no resistance being encountered. Once again, the assault force assembled in multiple vehicles and collected their weapons near to their target site. Once again, despite ostensible TTPS Special Branch surveillance, the Jamaat was able to assemble unimpeded.

Within TTT, senior journalist Jones P. Madiera was confronted by the sight of gunmen in the building and, along with veteran journalist Raoul Pantin, was made to lie on the floor while the other employees of TTT were assembled by the assault group. Initially, there was speculation that it was an armed robbery until the arrival of Imam Abu Bakr. All women and children were allowed to leave along with two German technicians present on a training course. However, 26 hostages were held by the Jamaat-al-Muslimeen at TTT.[50]

Following the capture of the country's sole television station, the stage was set. It was at about 6:20 p.m. that the Imam Abu Bakr made his now famous (or infamous) broadcast:

> Good evening, ladies and gentlemen. We would like to take this opportunity to inform you that at about 6.00 p.m. this afternoon the Government of Trinidad and Tobago has been overthrown. The Prime Minister and members of the Cabinet are at present under arrest. The military are in contact with us and we are asking everybody to lay down their arms so that there can be a peaceful transition. We're asking people not to involve in looting or any form of unlawful actions or else they will have to pay the consequences thereof. We would like to keep you informed with a further news broadcast as we proceed.[51]

The TTDF Reacts

The TTDF was, like all agencies, caught unawares but reacted quite quickly within its limited resources and its lack of prior experience in these matters. In this regard, the football match referred to earlier, offered the regiment quite a bit of assistance. The CO TTR, Colonel Ralph Brown, was at the said match when at 6:00 p.m., minutes after the attack began, he was informed by one Felix Hernandez and, after gathering all members of the TTR and TTDF who had gathered there, left immediately for the TTR's small base, Camp Ogden, located in St James, near Port of Spain.[52]

Colonel Brown recalled that one of the first things he did on hearing of this was to request all members of the TTR to leave the stadium and assemble, making the announcement over the stadium's public address system.[53] Nearly 200 TTR soldiers had been issued passes to the football game and were available at short notice.[54]

By 6:15 p.m., Captain Rodney Smart had 'closed the gates' and confined the personnel at both Camp Ogden and the TTR's forward base for anti-marijuana operations at Camp Cumuto. In terms of available forces, the TTR had one sub-strength rifle company deployed at Camp Cumuto, 60 personnel from both the TTR and TTCG were gathered from the football match and despatched to Camp Ogden, plus whatever personnel were in camp at the time. Available forces were aided by the recent induction of four hundred privates into the TTR over a period of 12 months.[55]

While CO 1st Battalion TTR, Lieutenant Colonel Hugh Vidal, despatched two officers to ascertain what was happening, Colonel Joseph Theodore, the Chief of Defence Staff, having also been apprised of the situation, despatched two warrant officers for a similar fact-finding mission. At this point, neither Colonels Brown nor Theodore or any of their subordinates had an inkling of a hostage situation being evident with only the bombing of the TTPS HQ and gunfire being then known.[56]

At about 7:00 p.m. Colonel Brown was able to return from his football game to the forward TTR post at Camp Ogden and there he met Colonel Theodore and Lieutenant Colonel Vidal. At this point they waited for the nightly television news at 7:00 p.m., which is something of an institution in Trinidad, more so in 1990, but it was only at about 7:15 p.m. that they saw Imam Abu Bakr appear on television with the dawning realisation that the TTT studios had been seized by the Jamaat. Colonel Brown at 7:30 p.m. gave Major Joseph orders to secure the Nelson Exchange of the Trinidad and Tobago telephone company to ensure no misuse of the communications network.[57]

Within its resources, the TTR moved as quickly as possible to contain the Jamaat within a limited geographic area and had done so with forces at its disposal, which were, admittedly very limited. Camp Ogden was to prove a rallying point for military personnel but was neither stocked nor provisioned to properly outfit such forces and the fact that Major Joseph could only assemble the equivalent of a rifle platoon a full hour after Camp Ogden was closed and personnel confined, illustrates problems faced in generating combat units.

Of equal importance, however, is the poor level of communications and coordination between the individual battalions and sometimes individual officers. Fortunately, this did not have a major impact owing to the overall incompetence of the Jamaat and the fact that the insurrection was geographically contained quite quickly. This unfortunate state of affairs could have led to major problems as communications between the 1st Infantry Battalion and the 2nd Service and Support Battalion were particularly poor for the first 48 hours and the TTCG was not even informed until sometime later and was largely left to operate as it deemed fit.

The CO of the TTCG, Commander Kelshall, was not informed through official channels of the insurrection and was actually informed by his mother-in-law about the apparent attack on TTPS HQ and the subsequent address to the nation by Imam Abu Bakr.[58] He took care to secure the assets of the TTCG, perhaps fearful of an attack on the TTCG HQ at Staubles Bay or its subsidiary base at Harts Cut. This was by way of guaranteeing the security of the forces at his command. By way of specific tactical responses, the CO TTCG did the following:

secured the Coast Guard Station
instructed the Coast Guard vessels to carry out area patrols
set up road blocks
seized the heliport in Chaguaramas
established patrols
took over assets at Piarco airport where the Air Wing was based[59]

These responses were undoubtedly sound and well-reasoned. However, Commander Kelshall took the additional step of bringing his Special Naval Unit to a high state of alert and used it to bolster the security of his Coast Guard facilities, augmenting the armed ratings already deployed for that task.[60] Much effort was expended setting up machine gun nests and roadblocks around TTCG bases and moving ammunition on board TTCG vessels CG-4, CG-5 and CG-6.[61]

It was not until 7:30 p.m. that Colonel Brown spoke with him and, recognising the need for reinforcements, members of the Special Naval Unit were despatched to Port of Spain, with TTCG vehicles assisting in transporting ammunition to the TTR.[62]

Later, at the request of Colonel Theodore, Commander Kelshall deployed CG-4 (TTS *Buccoo Reef*), CG-5 (TTS *Barracuda*) and CG-6 (TTS *Cascadura*) to protect Port of Spain harbour and the Coast Guard bases at Hart's Cut and Staubles Bay.[63]

The TTCG's control of the Air Wing came to the fore when on Saturday morning, Lieutenant Commander Curtis Roach, Lieutenant Commander Bernard Baksh and retired Lieutenant Gaylord Kelshall came to Coast Guard Headquarters to offer their assistance. Lieutenant Kelshall, despite being long retired, was detailed to command the helicopters at the airport as he was the only military officer with aviation experience on hand. The civil helicopters of the National Helicopter Services Limited performed 46 military flights and were deployed to conduct reconnaissance and disperse looters.[64] In addition, the presence of the Coast Guard Air Wing, with its armed personnel at Piarco, enabled the airport to be secured relatively quickly once instructions were given, aided quite commendably by the airport's own security who acted to close the runway with efficiency.

The TTR found itself having to contain the Jamaat at the Red House, which was successfully done on the night of 27 July itself. Rather less successful, however, were attempts to contain and isolate the Jamaat at TTT and Radio Trinidad. This was largely due to a paucity of manpower and as will be noted was directly attributable to a failure of the TTPS to respond effectively to the situation and the inability of the Guard and Emergency Branch (GEB) of the TTPS to respond in any meaningful way to the insurrection or to effectively assist the TTR on that night. In fact, despite having a strength of several hundred personnel – armed and trained – the GEB was conspicuous by its absence on the first night of the insurrection and with the TTPS units in Port of Spain being largely unarmed, poorly trained and panicked after the destruction of their headquarters, the TTR found itself having to contend with the insurrection almost entirely on its own.

However, by the next day, reinforcements had arrived and the situation had largely stabilised as additional platoons from the TTR were able to secure perimeters around the TTT/ Radio Trinidad

TTR troops with SLRs using Trinidad and Tobago Electricity Commission vehicles. (Gayelle TV)

A Shorland armoured car and Shorland APC, as deployed in 1990. (Gayelle TV)

compounds and thus, in three locations, were able to completely isolate the Jamaat units from mutually supporting each other. This was a major factor in containing the military situation and it speaks to the amateurish nature of the insurrection and the limited resources of the TTPS, that a force of 114 insurgents was effectively contained by two platoons – about 60 men – of the TTR by the early hours of 28 July.

The military operations between 28 July and 1 August 1990 were quite anti-climactic in many ways as that early operation with 60 men effectively turned the insurrection into a combination of a siege and hostage situation. The operations also speak highly of the motivation and initiative taken by relatively junior officers in containing a force of unknown size.

Under orders, and in the early hours of 28 July, Captain George Clarke went with 22 men – a platoon minus – to an area west of the Queen's Park Savannah. This was done in order to secure a position around the Savannah and thereby dominate the area near to TTT. This unit was hastily put together and while they had rifles, basic kit and a load of ammunition, they did not necessarily have the weapons to which they were assigned. This force, however, was able to throw a cordon around TTT and establish and maintain a dominant presence in the area.[65]

Later that day, Saturday, 28th July, Major Joseph's troops came under heavy and sustained fire from the Jamaat forces in the Red House. As the TTR returned fire, an insurrectionist was shot trying to get into a vehicle outside the Red House. However, after Canon Knolly Clarke's intervention with the amnesty document described in the next chapter, at 6:00 p.m. Major Joseph was ordered to cease fire except if fired upon. However, members of the TTPS, once again displaying a lack of discipline, continued firing from the Cyril Duprey building apparently in defiance of orders from the Acting Commissioner of Police. A helicopter sortie established their presence and, after polite requests to get them to cease failed, Colonel Theodore threatened to have his special forces 'take them out'. At that point the TTPS ceased firing.[66]

Reinforcements from Alpha Company under the command of Major Ancil Antione arrived to reinforce Captain Clarke by noon on Saturday. Under fire, these forces made a multi-pronged attack against the Jamaat forces at TTT and were able to force the Jamaat into the TTT building and confine them there, thus totally containing the Jamaat at that location, injuring four insurrectionists in the process. Once again soon after 6:00 p.m., there was a ceasefire at TTT.[67]

With negotiations still going on, Major Joseph ordered a B-300 rocket to be launched against the Red House at an area away from the area of the parliamentary chamber where the hostages were held. This was done on Sunday morning when the Jamaat insurrectionists attempted a breakout from the Red House and engaged the TTR in a heavy gun battle. The B-300 caused a small fire that was easily extinguished by the Jamaat.[68]

The next day, on Monday afternoon, Captain Clarke's troops outside TTT directed heavy fire against the building and, even up to Tuesday, there were sporadic exchanges of gunfire between the TTR and the Jamaat. During this time, negotiations were continuing; the Prime Minister had been released and the release of all hostages was by then anticipated.[69]

However, on Wednesday, 1 August 1990 – the very day of release and surrender – Captain Clarke launched a B300 rocket against the TTT building. This was done ostensibly because Clarke wanted to 'test the capability of the building to withstand any attempt to penetrate it' and to remind the Jamaat that '... they were in a war'. Captain Clarke's actions, which had hitherto been exemplary was severely criticised for using the B-300 in such an apparently reckless manner.[70]

The insurrection left 24 people dead and 231 wounded, 133 of them in an orgy of looting and arson that followed leading to losses amounting to hundreds of millions of dollars.[71] Popular support for the insurrection was minimal but a total breakdown in law enforcement led to chaos, exploited by looters for personal gain. While the insurrection ended with the surrender of Bakr and his followers, they were acquitted of charges brought against them in the Trinidadian courts, which upheld an amnesty granted to them to secure the lives of the hostages. This has emboldened them and Bakr and his adherents have continued to occupy an important position of influence and prominence in the local Islamic community and the local criminal community.

The TTDF Today

Table 21: TTDF strength

	Total Strength	Army	Air Force	Coast Guard
Active personnel	4,657	2,680	420	1,557
Reserves	400 (full-time) and 224 (part-time)	400	80	144

The Trinidad and Tobago Regiment

The TTR has been the senior formation in the TTDF – despite its 1970 mutiny and slow rehabilitation thereafter – and has had a major share of personnel to date. The TTR is organised into four battalions – two infantry, one engineer, and one service and support. It currently lacks armour as its Shorland armoured cars and personnel carriers are now all derelict. Neither does it have any artillery beyond a single mortar platoon with 81mm mortars which were effectively non-operational until 2019 after being in storage for nearly 20 years for want of trained personnel.

The TTR is an infantry and support force with only soft-skinned vehicles for transport. The TTR lacks any ability to defend Trinidad's territorial integrity from foreign aggression and is not configured for a dedicated counter-insurgency function either. While the TTR has grown in size, its equipment has not kept pace with this expansion and with neither armour nor support weapons, the TTR is actually less well-equipped than it was in 1990 in some key respects. Israeli small arms – Galils and Negevs – dominate the inventory with the H&K MP5 and UMP being the principal submachine guns and 7.62mm GPMGs providing company and platoon level support.

In 2014–2015 there were some attempts to procure a force of APCs for the TTDF. In 2009, the requirement was set at a total of 19 APCs but no progress was made despite a number of wheeled internal security APCs being shortlisted for procurement. The entire proposal was shelved in 2016 and has not been resurrected. With no armour, no artillery and support weapons being limited to some company level 60mm mortars of questionable utility, a reactivated Support Weapons Detachment operating the 81mm mortars and a limited number of .50 Browning M2HB heavy machine guns alongside GPMGs of the M60 and FN MAG types, the TTDF is effectively a force of lightly armed infantry and is in dire need of an infusion of new equipment.

The TTCG – Recapitalised but Still Crippled

After a number of years with almost no serviceable vessels, the period 1999–2001 saw the TTCG receive a boost with the acquisition of the ex-Royal Navy Island-class OPV, HMS *Orkney* renamed TTS *Nelson* (CG-20) and four 82ft Point-class cutters, each displacing some 66 tonnes, from the United States (TTS *Corozal Point* CG7, TTS *Crown Point* CG8, TTS *Galera Point* CG9 and TTS *Bacolet Point CG10*). The Point-class cutters were nominally on strength until 2009–2010 when they were decommissioned but, in reality, they had been unseaworthy for some years prior. A half-hearted attempt was made to refit CG-7 but was abandoned It is a depressing fact that these vessels were well over 20 years old when procured. The stark reality was that not a single new-build patrol vessel was acquired between 1980 and 2009.[72]

In 2003–2004, the then government of Patrick Manning began a phased expansion of the formation which included the purchase of six new Austal PB30 Fast Patrol Craft (FPC) – CG11 TTS *Scarlet Ibis*, CG12 TTS *Hibiscus*, CG13 TTS *Humming Bird*, CG14 TTS *Chaconia*, CG 15 TTS *Poui* and CG16 TTS *Teak* – commissioned between 2009 and 2010, and two modified oil rig support vessels – each over 15 years old – armed and re-tasked as coastal patrol vessels (CPVs) – CG-21 TTS *Gaspar Grande* and CG-22 TTS

Point-class cutters GG-10 and CG-9. (TTCG)

Modified Spica-class vessel CG-6, TTS *Cascadura*. (TTCG)

CG-14, an Austal APB-30. (Austal)

CG-14 in 2013 – in very poor condition. (Photo by Author)

CG-6, TTS Cascadura. (TTCG)

Chacachare – commissioned on 23 April 2008. In addition, four Midnight Express Interceptors were delivered in 2005 and were extensively deployed in anti-narcotics operations.

The Austal APB 30s (CG-11 to CG-16) which were delivered between 2009 and 2010 experienced severe problems in Trinidadian service. The aluminium hulls of the vessels proved to be wholly inadequate for operations on the country's northern coast and severe problems were experienced with marine growth. Between 2010 and 2015, the Austal FPB 30s were the country's main maritime assets and they were tasked with roles for which they were not designed, placing undue stress on their somewhat delicate construction. Rather more puzzling were persistent electronic failures with radar and FLIR systems becoming unserviceable at an unusually high rate – only one of the two radars aboard usually being operational at any time.[73]

The 'crown jewels' of this expansion plan were three 90m-long OPVs – to be named the *Port of Spain, Scarborough* and *San Fernando* – ordered from VT Shipbuilding (later BAE Systems Surface Ships). Easily the most advanced vessels in the Caribbean (after the demise of the Cuban navy), the OPVs were adequately armed with 25mm and 30mm guns and possessed the ability to stage medium-lift helicopters from their flight decks. However, an overly ambitious integrated fire-control system and some unrealistic expectations from the TTCG in respect of the performance of the 30mm guns led to significant delays and problems during trials. In September 2010, the government of the then Prime Minister Kamla Persad-Bissessar cancelled the contract, a decision that in retrospect may have been ill-advised.

Of interest is the fact that the procurement of new vessels did not lead to a commensurate increase in the TTCG operational budget relative to the larger fleet. In addition, archaic bureaucratic procedures together with shortcomings in the TTCG engineering and maintenance branches combined to cripple efforts to restore serviceability to repairable vessels with contractors being unpaid for work done and vessels being laid-up for extended periods of time.

The Damen Acquisition – FCS 5009s and SPa 5009s

After deliberating and assessing the vessels and designs on offer, four CPVs were acquired from the Dutch shipyard, Damen, with two additional vessels of a similar design being acquired as 'utility vessels' but so armed and equipped that they could augment the four dedicated CPVs in the patrol role. The vessels selected were the SPa 5009 CPV and the FCS 5009 utility vessel. The CPVs were fitted with a surveillance system which drew heavily on high-end civilian products. In addition, they were fitted with a remotely controlled 20mm gun. The FCS 5009 was delivered in standard configuration but with accommodation increased for a larger crew, a manually operated 20mm gun (from TTCG stocks) and a slightly enhanced surveillance fit.

The two FCS 5009s were ordered as they were available for rapid delivery – sea trials taking place in December 2014. However, it was felt that the standard fit on the vessels was inadequate for the TTCG. In order to give the vessels more flexibility, the following modifications were made to the basic FCS 5009, aside from the necessary internal rearrangements to make them suitable for quasi-military use:

1) An adaptor for a GAM-B01 20mm gun was fitted forward. The wetness forward was not deemed an issue largely because any armed patrol duties were to be of a secondary nature to these vessels;

2) A Voyager II FLIR system was installed to provide a modicum of additional surveillance capability;

3) A Heila hydraulically operated knuckle-boom crane was installed which had the secondary function of being able to lower and recover a DI 1102 interceptor.[74]

The remains of CG-6. (Photo by Author)

CG-26, TTS *Quinam* of the Damen SPa 5009-class. (Photo by Author)

These two vessels – CG 23 TTS *Point Lisas* and CG 24 TTS *Brighton* – were delivered in the period May/June 2015 and duly commissioned into the TTCG.

The TTCG's SPa 5009s are easily the best equipped naval vessels in the English-speaking Caribbean. Unique among the ships of the region, they have a Combat Information Centre (CIC). The CIC housed displays – Transas NS4100s surveillance workstations – showing the radar, WECDIS and FLIR input with repeaters on the bridge. It was also envisaged that the CIC would house a dedicated secure communications suite supplied by Harris. Deliveries of the Harris equipment were delayed, leading to the vessels being commissioned without this equipment being fitted.[75]

The surveillance fit selected was a compromise using high quality civilian systems as opposed to dedicated military systems. The surveillance radar selected was the Kelvin Hughes X-Band Sharp Eye which emerged as the most cost-effective and available choice. The FLIR system chosen was the MU602CLW. A Saab R5 data link was also fitted along with a Rotheta RT-500M radio direction finder. It should be noted that the TTCG had expressed a desire for a Terma surveillance radar as fitted to the BAES OPVs. However, cost factors militated against this.

To enhance the interdiction capabilities of the SPa 5009, the standard stern-launched MST 750SR 7.5m RHIB was supplemented by a davit launched DI 1102 interceptor. While it was intended that the interceptor be launched and recovered while the mother vessel was moving, two incidents during familiarisation training may have led to a rethink in this regard.

The choice of weapon fell to the Rheinmetall/MSI Seahawk LW20A1 system. This proved to be a somewhat problematic choice as two rounds of firing trials – one in 2015 and one in 2016 – were aborted due to severe malfunctions. Even during those aborted trials, however, the accuracy of the system was excellent, but the aborted trials delayed the operationalisation of the vessels' weapons systems until late 2016.[76]

Owing to somewhat delayed payments, the four SPa 5009s were delivered between 2015 and 2016 and were designated and named as follows: CG 25 TTS *Speyside*, CG 26 TTS *Quinam*, CG 27 TTS *Moruga* and CG 28 TTS *Carli Bay*. Each of these vessels carried a DI 1102 interceptor, with two more being deployable on CG 23 and CG 24.

The LRPV procurement was not so fortunate as it was circumvented by the direct intervention of the then Prime Minister Persad-Bissessar who decided, against advice, to procure a ready-made, unarmed LRPV from CSSC of China which compared badly with the cancelled OPVs. The vessel procured, commissioned as CG-60, TTS *Nelson II*, was the largest military vessel in the English-speaking Caribbean but had very limited capabilities. Its surveillance system was not up to the standard.

By the end of 2016, from contracts signed under the People's Partnership government, the Coast Guard had:

- One 79m Chinese-made LRPV
- Four 50m Damen SPa 5009 CPVs
- Two 50m Damen FCS 5009 armed utility vessels
- Two 46m legacy CPVs returned to service.
- Six legacy Austal APB 30 Fast Patrol Craft (of dubious serviceability)
- Six DI 1102 onboard interceptors
- Seventeen legacy interceptors (four of which were operational)
- Six pirogues[77]

Serviceability problems have bedevilled the interceptor fleet but some efforts to restore unserviceable vessels have shown results but, even now, only six or eight of the 17 interceptors are operational. The 79m Chinese OPV has been largely inoperable since 2017.

However, the Damen patrol fleet has been experiencing a spate of maintenance problems, compounded by the temporary withdrawal of Dutch technicians due to the Wuhan Coronavirus pandemic. The

Table 22: The TTCG Fleet Today

Class	Manufacturer	Role	Original total	In service	Commissioned
Nelson II (ex-Haijian 1001)	Huangpu Shipyard	Offshore patrol vessel	1	1	2015
Cape-class	Austal	Offshore/Coastal Patrol Vessel	2	2	2021
Gaspar Grande	VT Shipbuilding	Coastal patrol vessel	2	2	2008
APB 30	Austal	Patrol craft	6	0	2009
Fast Crew Supplier 5009	Damen	Utility and Patrol Vessel	2	2	2015
Stan Patrol 5009	Damen	Coastal Patrol Vessel	4	4	2015
Interception Craft 1102	Damen	Interceptor craft	6	6*	2015
Bowen	n/k	Interceptor craft	2	0	1991
Midnight Express	Midnight Express	Interceptor craft	2	2 (unserviceable)	2005
Formula 111	n/k	Interceptor craft	2	2 (unserviceable)	2005
Phantom Enforcer Edgewater	Phantom	Interceptor craft Interceptor craft	3 2	3 (questionable serviceability) 2 (questionable serviceability)	n/k
Reform	n/k	Auxiliary vessel	1	0 (prison ship, unserviceable)	n/k

* Only six DI 1102 were purchased – four are mounted aboard the SPa 5009s and two can be carried aboard the FCS 5009s. There is reluctance to deploy the DI 1102s after a series of nearly fatal accidents.

expiration of the maintenance contract with Damen in 2021 may compound these problems. However, as of April 2021, all six Damen 50m vessels are operational.

The purchase of two Austal Cape-class patrol boats in 2018 will add to the existing fleet but it is unclear as to what role they would fulfil, being somewhat less capable than the SPa 5009 fleet in the CPV role but lacking the range to make them OPVs. These two Cape-class vessels are due to enter service in 2021 and the TTCG took delivery of CG 41 TTS *Port of Spain* and CG 42 TTS *Scarborough* on 14 May 2021.[78]

The first vessel – CG 41 – was launched by Austal on 3 December 2020, after a substantial delay occasioned by the Wuhan Coronavirus and its effect upon the operations of the shipyard. The contract was for AU$ 126 million, which would approximate to US$ 49 million per vessel with its attendant support package. These vessels mark the first export of the Cape-class, with the type having only been supplied to Australian agencies to date. Austal described the Trinidadian vessels in the following terms:

> The new TTCG *Capes* are based on the 58 metre aluminium monohull patrol boat, first developed by Austal in Australia for Australian Border Force. The vessels have a 4,000 nautical mile range and 28-day patrol cycle, with a crew of up to 22. Each *Cape* is equipped with two high-speed 7.3 metre rigid hull inflatable boats used for intercepting other vessels.[79]

Damen-built SPa 5009 TTS *Quinam* of the *Trinidad* and Tobago Coast Guard. (Damen Shipyards)

Two SPa 5009s of the TTCG – TTS *Moruga* and TTS *Carli Bay*, before departure to Trinidad. (Damen Shipyards)

In addition to its vessels, Trinidad and Tobago possesses an excellent coastal radar network with Elta El/M-2226 radars around the country's coast and also covers the islands of St Vincent and Grenada. While there have been occasional serviceability issues, these radars are functional and are being upgraded. This radar network has not prevented a thriving enterprise in smuggling illegal Venezuelan economic migrants, illegal weapons and narcotics from South America to Trinidad.

Air Arms – Growth and Decline

Trinidad and Tobago had no air force yet has one of the Commonwealth Caribbean's largest air arms comprising two separate entities – the Trinidad and Tobago Air Guard and the National Operations Centre Air Division. For a country with decidedly limited numbers of air assets, having two organisations has led to duplication of effort and a faulty procurement process that has ensured no compatibility of either aircraft or avionics.[80]

The Trinidad and Tobago Air Guard

The Trinidad and Tobago Air Guard (TTAG) as an independent service has had a very short life, being formed in 2005 by Cabinet Minute #1936 dated 28 July 2005 and inherited the force of the old TTCG Air Wing – two Piper Navajos, one Cessna 310, one Cessna 402 and two C-26s.[81]

The Cessna 402 was withdrawn from service in 1998 but again remained in the hangar on supports for at least two years. The late 1990s, however, were to bring a fresh lease of life to the outfit. At a time of enhanced counter-narcotics cooperation between the United States and Trinidad, the sight of US DEA Blackhawk helicopters was common at the Air Wing's base and in exchange, the United States transferred two seized PA-31 Piper Navajos (serials 203 and 204) and two Swearingen C-26A Metro aircraft (serials 215 and 216) to the Air Wing, thus infusing the stagnating outfit with new capabilities.

The Navajos, after becoming unserviceable (the bane of Trinidadian military equipment) were phased out in 2009–2010 but the C-26As form the most potent fixed wing assets of the force, renamed the Air Guard in 2005. C-26A serial 216 has been fitted with MR radar and FLIR while 215 appears to serve in the transport role capable of carrying 14 troops as far as Puerto Rico – a useful capability when handling disaster relief operations within the Caribbean.

TTS *Carli Bay* during trials. (Damen Shipyards)

Damen-manufactured FCS 5009 TTS *Brighton*, during trials. (Damen Shipyards)

A left-hand view of the C-26 light transport of the Trinidad and Tobago Coast Guard Air Wing. (Photo by Author)

The fixed wing assets of the TTAG, therefore, were limited to three serviceable and notionally operational aircraft – two C-26As and one Cessna 310. Total flight time in 2008–2009 was over 250 hours in 121 missions – a figure substantially lower than the norm in 2000–2001 when over 350 hours were logged. This figure fell further by 2012 when the Cessna 310 was withdrawn from service without replacement. In addition, the C-26 aircraft began to show their age and equipment problems with the Elta M-2022 radar on board aircraft 216 seriously compromising the efficacy in the vital maritime surveillance role. Acute shortages of spares compounded a major serviceability problem that has only been partially alleviated through a somewhat uneasy partnership with the Canadian company, Provincial Aerospace Limited.[82]

The TTAG received its rotary wing assets in the form of four AW139s (9Y-AG311, 9Y-AG312, 9Y-AG313 and 9Y-AG314) helicopters which were delivered between 2011 and 2012. Costing over US$ 200 million, these four helicopters were plagued with a series of problems including structural cracks in their tail booms and required very delicate handling in air-conditioned hangars thus placing a heavy strain on the TTAG's limited infrastructure.

Exacerbating the problem was the fact that the TTAG had no trained helicopter pilots and was forced to employ foreign civilian pilots on contract while building flying hours for local pilots under some very generous contracts which worked to the detriment of the TTAG. The net result was that the helicopters remained severely restricted operationally, until their grounding in 2017.[83]

Almost completely neglected in the discourse on military aviation in Trinidad is the long-suffering C-26 fleet. The need for a replacement is acute as the aircraft are currently operating on borrowed time as spares and support for the type become ever more difficult to obtain. Furthermore, the maritime surveillance role performed by these aircraft is crucial to the country's border security and as these aircraft become progressively less serviceable, a huge gap will emerge in Trinidad's maritime domain awareness.

The National Operations Centre Air Division

Between 2010 and 2015, the NOC Air Division was a favoured outfit and received lavish budgetary attention perhaps in part because of its role in performing VIP transport missions for the then government of Prime Minister Kamla Persad-Bissessar. The NOC Air Division inherited assets from a defunct unit called the Special Anti-Crime Unit of Trinidad and Tobago (SAUTT), which operated at its zenith

Another look at the sole C-26 of the TTCG Air Wing. (Photo by Author)

four helicopters – one S-76A+, one AS.355 and two BO-105 CBS-4 – and a Westinghouse Skyship 600.

The aircraft were equipped with FLIR turrets on external pylons and Night-Sun searchlights. The S-76 and BO-105s were natural choices for SAUTT as the country has a long history of operating these types through its civilian National Helicopter Services Limited (NHSL).[84]

For Trinidad and Tobago to operate two separate air arms with no equipment compatibility makes no sense. It can be argued that the procurement of AW139s for the TTAG made little sense given NHSL's successful record with S-76s and BO-105s. This situation was exacerbated by a combination of economic hardship occasioned by a fall in the price of oil as well as the high maintenance costs of some of the assets.

Helicopter Assets – Growth and Decline

The Trinidad and Tobago Air Guard (TTAG) acquired four AW139 helicopters in the period 2010–2011. However, on 29 June 2017, in an unexpected decision, especially after investing over US$ 348 million in the acquisition of the helicopters and the training of personnel, the government of Trinidad and Tobago decided that it could no longer afford the annual maintenance costs of the helicopters amounting to some US$ 29 million.[85] Despite the fact that the TTAG's AW139 squadron had won awards for humanitarian assistance, and despite two previous administrations being committed to keeping the aircraft airworthy, the cost of maintaining the helicopters was deemed excessive.[86]

Since the TTAG remained entirely dependent on external contractors for the maintenance of the AW139s, they have been grounded since June 2017 in a closed hangar at the Ulric Cross Air Station at Piarco International Airport. To add to the ignominy, the government of Trinidad and Tobago was sued by Cobham, the company tasked with maintaining the AW139s, and failed to file a defence leading to the government having to pay US$ 10 million plus costs for a maintenance contract for helicopters that were unnecessarily grounded. In 2021, an attempt was made to reactivate one AW139 and the aircraft received certification from the country's Civil Aviation Authority, but none of the TTAG pilots are now current on type, most having left.

This decision has effectively meant the grounding of the TTAG as its two ageing C-26 aircraft are rarely operational and in dire need of replacement. The inability of Trinidad to create a local maintenance infrastructure has now come to haunt the TTAG and its existence may be doubtful as a separate establishment.

While the TTAG grapples to justify its existence, the National Operations Centre Air Division is facing severe challenges of its own. Flying hours have been savagely cut from over three hundred hours per year on average per pilot, to under one hundred with standing air surveillance patrols coming to a halt.[87] While at least part of the reduction in flying hours has been caused by curtailing the use of the NOC Air Division helicopters as VIP transports, the cuts to air patrols have proved to be detrimental to the unit's response time to incidents.

The efficiency of the helicopter fleet has been worsened by the failure to completely integrate Harris secure communications suites before the removal of earlier Motorola equipment leading to a virtual breakdown in real-time communication between the Air Division's helicopters and ground units. In addition, and somewhat inexplicably, the night-surveillance systems fitted to the NOC's AS.355 and two BO-105 helicopters are now non-operational and have been removed from the aircraft pending repairs which have not taken place to date – the equipment remaining in boxes at the Air Division's base in Central Trinidad.

An attempt to replace the NOC Air Division's ageing assets with a new fleet of four Bell 429 and one Bell 412EPI helicopters has become embroiled in a dispute with the government facing legal action over non-payment for both the helicopters and a special hangar for the aircraft.[88] Compounding these equipment issues was the non-payment of salaries to pilots which led to a 'sick-out' by aircrew, effectively grounding the Air Division briefly while the government sought to make the requisite payments.[89] The whole process culminated in the non-renewal of pilot contracts and the subsequent re-hiring of a few with the attendant disruption to services.

With the grounding of the AW139s, the NOC Air Division was transferred to the Trinidad and Tobago Air Guard. However, one of its S-76A++ helicopters has been

Table 23: Trinidad and Tobago's Air Assets

Platform family	Platform variant	Primary role (general)	Primary role (specific)	Estimated in service	First delivery date
Metro	C-26B	Maritime	Patrol	2	1999
One of the aircraft is equipped with Elta M-2022 radar and FLIR.					
AW139	AW139	Logistics	Utility	4 (withdrawn from use and grounded)	2011
AS.355F2	Ecureuil	Logistics	Utility	1	n/k
Sikorsky 76A	Sikorsky 76A	Logistics	Utility	1 grounded	n/k
BO-105CBS-4	BO-105CBS-4	Logistics	Utility	2	n/k

Austal Cape-class vessel TTS *Port of Spain*. (Austal)

grounded for over five years awaiting an autopilot, while a leased S-76D is now subject to legal proceedings after the government of Dr Keith Rowley refused to honour a lease executed by his opposition rival when she was Prime Minister. Of the remaining helicopters, only one AS.355 and one BO-105 are operational with another BO-105 being used as a spares source for the single operational machine of that type. Thus, from a fleet of ten helicopters in 2015, Trinidad has been reduced to two operational helicopters available for security operations, and these two lack surveillance equipment.

Conclusion

The TTDF is in dire need of a revamp, with reform and reorientation being necessary. However, with a very delicate internal security situation, the TTDF finds itself unable to carry out the reforms and reorientation that it knows to be necessary. Even the valid argument that a stronger TTCG which can seal off the import routes for weapons and narcotics and so rob the gangs of their financial resources and "muscle" has failed to make the necessary impact among decision makers. To them, the need to have the visible presence of the TTR in the fight against criminal gangs, owing to the inadequacies of the TTPS, takes priority and, as such, instituting reforms and reorienting the TTDF remains an aspiration that seems unlikely to be fulfilled.

The TTDF is a relatively large force, perhaps the largest in the Caribbean, but its efficacy has been crippled by an ad hoc procurement policy and a very casual, if not nonsensical approach to maintaining its assets. It also suffers from poor levels of accountability and lacks both the human and material resources to reach its full potential. It is replete with assets it cannot maintain and does not use efficiently. These shortcomings limit the utility of the force as a combat unit.

However, it should also be noted that this same force rose to the occasion when it was needed most desperately in 1990. Since the unfortunate events of 1970, the TTDF has shown itself to be fiercely committed to the Trinidadian Constitution and is a force with considerable potential to become more potent. While its challenges and limitations are well known, its positives of professionalism, an apolitical approach to its duties and its willingness to be an effective aid to the civil authority, stand it in good stead.

SELECT BIBLIOGRAPHY

Adkin, Mark, *Urgent Fury: The Battle for Grenada* (London: Leo Cooper, 1989)

Conway's All the World's Fighting Ships 1947-1995 (London, Conway Maritime Press: 1995)

Danns, G.K., *Domination and Power in Guyana* (New Brunswick: Transaction Books, 1982)

Disciplined Forces Commission Report (May 2004)

Furlonge-Kelly, E.T.V., *The Silent Victory* (Port of Spain: Golden Eagle, 1991)

Griffith, Ivelaw Lloyd, *Drugs and Security in the Caribbean: Sovereignty Under Siege* (Pennsylvania: Penn State Press: 1997)

Griffith, Ivelaw Lloyd, *The Quest for Security in the Caribbean: Problems and Promises in Subordinate States* (New York: M.E. Sharpe, 1993)

Hylton-Edwards, Stewart, *Lengthening Shadows: Birth and Revolt of the Trinidad Army* (Port of Spain: Inprint Caribbean: 1982)

Joint History Office of the Chairman of the Joint Chiefs of Staff *Operation Urgent Fury* (CreateSpace Independent Publishing Platform 2014)

Liverpool, Compton Hartley, *Foundation of the Guyana Defence Force: A Soldier of Valour Story* (AuthorHouse 2016; Kindle Edition)

O'Dowd, D.J., *Review of the Trinidad and Tobago Police Service* (Unpublished, May 1991)

Raines, Edgar F., *The Rucksack War* (Washington: Center for Military History, 2010)

Russell, Lee E. & Albert Mendez, M., *Grenada 1983* (London: Osprey, 1983)

Shah, Raffique, 'The People Have Absolved Me', in S. Ryan (ed.), Power: The Black Power Revolution 1970 (St Augustine: ISER, 1995)

Ryan, S., *The Muslimeen Grab for Power* (Port of Spain: Inprint, 1991)

Singh, C., *Guyana: Politics in a Plantation Society* (Stanford: Praeger Publ. 1988)

Trinidad and Tobago Parliament, *Report of the Commission of Enquiry into the 1990 attempted coup*, http://ttparliament.org/documents/rptcoe1990.pdf

Trinidad Under Siege (Daily Express 1990)

West Kingston Commission of Inquiry

NOTES

Chapter 1

1 Oscar Ramjeet, 'CARICOM Countries Will Speak With One Voice in Meetings With US And Canadian Leaders', *Caribbean Net News* (17 April 2009)http://www.caribbeannewsnow.com/caribnet/caricom/caricom.php?news_id=15757&start=440&category_id=39> accessed 8 Jul. 2016.

2 Sue Ann Wayow, 'Here's why T&T should pay attention to Brexit', *Trinidad Express* (24 June 2016), <http://www.trinidadexpress.com/20160624/business/heres-why-tt-should-pay-attention-to-brexit>, accessed 8 Jul. 2016.

3 'Countries and Regions – Caribbean', *European Commission*, <http://ec.europa.eu/trade/policy/countries-and-regions/regions/caribbean/>, accessed 8 Jul. 2021.

4 'Trinidad and Tobago PM hails Chinese dream', *China Daily Europe* (2 June 2013), <http://europe.chinadaily.com.cn/china/2013-06/02/content_16556395.htm>, accessed 1 Aug. 2016.

5 Robin Wigglesworth, 'Caribbean in crisis: Chequebook diplomacy', *Financial Times* (17 December 2013), <https://www.ft.com/content/7f7b0d8e-5ea8-11e3-8621-00144feabdc0>, accessed 1 Aug. 2016.

6 Robin Wigglesworth, 'Caribbean in crisis: Chequebook diplomacy'.

7 'About Us', *Regional Security System*, <https://www.rss.org.bb/about-us/>.

8 'Regional Security System', *Aeroflight*, <http://www.aeroflight.co.uk/ops/mil/regional-security-system.htm>.

9 Lee E. Russell & M. Albert Mendez, *Grenada 1983* (London: Osprey, 1983), pp.5–7 and pp.45–46.

10 Report on "Operation Carib" prepared by Colonel H.D. Maynard (23 August 1990).

11 Report on "Operation Carib".

12 Report on "Operation Carib".

13 Report on "Operation Carib".

14 Report on "Operation Carib".

15 Sanjay Badri-Maharaj, 'The Response of CARICOM Armed Forces to Hurricane Maria', *IDSA* (6 December 2017), <https://www.idsa.in/idsacomments/the-response-of-caricom-armed-forces-to-hurricane-maria_sbmaharaj_061217>

16 'CARICOM says Dominica getting strong regional support', *Stabroek News* (25 September 2017), <https://www.stabroeknews.com/2017/news/regional/09/25/caricom-says-dominica-getting-strong-regional-support/>, accessed 5 Dec. 2017.

17 'JDF disaster assistance team deployed to Dominica', *Jamaica Observer* (26 September 2017), <http://www.jamaicaobserver.com/latestnews/JDF_disaster_assistance_team_deployed_to_Dominica?profile=1228>, accessed 5 Dec. 2017.

18 'JDF DART in Dominica', *Jamaica Defence Force* (Facebook: 10 October 2017), <https://www.facebook.com/jdfsoldier/videos/10154798333461384/>, accessed 5 Dec. 2017.

19 Julia Rawlings-Bentham, 'A long road to recovery for Dominica', *Caribbean News Now* (28 September 2017), <http://wp.caribbeannewsnow.com/2017/09/28/long-road-recovery-dominica/>, accessed 5 Dec. 2017.

20 Sasha Harrinanan, 'Coast Guard provides swift aid to Dominica', *Trinidad Newsday* (22 September 2017), <http://newsday.co.tt/2017/09/22/coast-guard-provides-swift-aid-to-dominica/>, accessed 5 Dec. 2017.

21 'T&T Coast Guard vessel leaves for Dominica with relief items', *Loop TT* (5 October 2017) <http://www.looptt.com/content/tt-coast-guard-vessel-leaves-dominica-relief-items>, accessed 5 Dec. 2017.

22 'TTS NELSON II LEAVES FOR DOMINICA', *Trinidad and Tobago* (Facebook: 10 October 2017) <https://www.facebook.com/pg/Trinidad-Tobago-Coast-Guard-621931181194075/photos/?tab=album&album_id=1480087155378469>, accessed 5 Dec. 2017.

23 'HMBS Lawrence Major arrives in Dominica', *Royal Bahamas Defence Force* (29 October 2017), <http://rbdf.gov.bs/hmbs-lawrence-major-arrives-in-dominica/>, accessed 5 Dec. 2017.
24 Robin Wigglesworth, 'Caribbean in crisis: Chequebook diplomacy'.
25 'China to sell long range border patrol vessel to TT', *Trinidad Express* (25 February 2014), <https://trinidadexpress.com/news/china-to-provide-long-range-border-patrol-vessel-to-tt-247051311.html>, accessed 1 Aug. 2016.
26 Between 1979 and 1983, Grenada was a recipient of substantial military largesse from the former Soviet Union and Cuba.
27 Sanjay Badri-Maharaj, 'Coast Guards in the Western Hemisphere – The Dutch Connection', *IDSA* (27 September 2016), <https://idsa.in/idsacomments/coast-guards-western-hemisphere-the-dutch-connection_sbmaharaj_270916>.

Chapter 2

1 *Conway's All the World's Fighting Ships 1947-1995* (London: Conway Maritime Press, 1995), p.21.
2 'The Flamingo Incident', *Royal Bahamas Defence Force*, <https://rbdf.gov.bs/the-flamingo-incident/>.
3 'The Flamingo Incident', *Royal Bahamas Defence Force*.
4 'New Entry Training', *Royal Bahamas Defence Force*, <https://rbdf.gov.bs/new-entry-training/#1536606570863-c90e43ad-e2b0>.
5 'Police uneasy at move to call in RBDF in crime fight', *The Tribune* (24 February 2017), <http://www.tribune242.com/news/2017/feb/24/police-uneasy-move-call-rbdf-crime-fight/>, and 'Police, Defence Force Crime Fight Collaboration "A Shared Vision"', *The Tribune* (24 February 2017),<http://www.tribune242.com/news/2017/feb/24/police-defence-force-crime-fight-collaboration-sha/>.
6 'Commando Training', *RBDF*, <https://rbdf.gov.bs/commando-training/>.
7 'Two armoured vehicles are delivered as a gift from China', *The Tribune* (4 May 2017), <http://www.tribune242.com/news/2017/may/04/two-armoured-vehicles-are-delivered-gift-china/>.
8 Li Jiyao, 'China donates military equipment to the Bahamas', *China Mail* (12 September 2017)< http://eng.chinamil.com.cn/view/2017-09/12/content_7752376.htm>.
9 Sanjay Badri-Maharaj, 'The Royal Bahamas Defence Force: Poised for Capability Growth', *IDSA* (30 November 2016), <https://idsa.in/idsacomments/royal-bahamas-defence-force_sbmaharaj_301116>.
10 Sanjay Badri-Maharaj, 'The Royal Bahamas Defence Force: Poised for Capability Growth'
11 Sanjay Badri-Maharaj, 'The Royal Bahamas Defence Force: Poised for Capability Growth', *IDSA* (30 November 2016), <https://idsa.in/idsacomments/royal-bahamas-defence-force_sbmaharaj_301116>.
12 Sanjay Badri-Maharaj, 'The Royal Bahamas Defence Force: Poised for Capability Growth'
13 Sanjay Badri-Maharaj, 'The Royal Bahamas Defence Force: Poised for Capability Growth', *IDSA* (30 November 2016), <https://idsa.in/idsacomments/royal-bahamas-defence-force_sbmaharaj_301116>.
14 'Royal Bahamas Defence Force', *Aeroflight*, <http://www.aeroflight.co.uk/tag/royal-bahamas-defence-force>.
15 'RBDF Conducts Aerial Drone training', *The Nassau Guardian*, <http://www.thenassauguardian.com/news/66343-rbdf-conducts-aerial-drone-training-exercise->.
16 'Bahamas Unmanned Aerial Systems (BUAS) Solution', <https://www.bahamas.gov.bs/wps/wcm/connect/85264722-4318-4e82-9739-a5c16f9fd3c3/BAHAMAS+UNMANNED+AERIAL+SYSTEMS+SOLUTION+-+RFP+EXTENDED+TIME.pdf?MOD=AJPERES>.
17 'Role of the Royal Bahamas Defence Force Prior to a Hurricane', *Royal Bahamas Defence Force* (Facebook: 27 April 2020), <https://www.facebook.com/RBDFMIL/posts/the-role-of-the-royal-bahamas-defence-force-prior-to-a-hurricanethe-hurricane-se/2879252135443994/>.
18 Sanjay Badri-Maharaj, 'The Royal Bahamas Defence Force Faces Criticisms post-Hurricane Dorian', <https://informesinbandera.com/noticias/The_Royal_Bahamas_Defence_Force_Faces_Criticisms_post-Hurricane_Dorian_51e337bc68c557c2506b126aeb045992>.

Chapter 3

1 Ivelaw Lloyd Griffith, *The Quest for Security in the Caribbean: Problems and Promises in Subordinate States* (New York: M.E. Sharpe, 1993), pp.118–119.
2 Ivelaw Lloyd Griffith, *The Quest for Security in the Caribbean: Problems and Promises in Subordinate States* (New York: M.E. Sharpe, 1993) pp.118–119.
3 Ivelaw Lloyd Griffith, *The Quest for Security in the Caribbean*, pp.118–119.
4 'Interview with former arms dealer, mercenary leader', *The Weekend Nation* (3 February 1984), pp.16–17.
5 Dion E Phillips, 'The Creation, Structure and Training of the Barbados Defense Force', *Caribbean Studies*, 21:1/2 (1988), p.134.
6 'About the Barbados Coast Guard', *Barbados Defence Force* <https://www.bdfbarbados.com/the-barbados-coast-guard/>, accessed 8 Jul. 2021.
7 *Conway's All the World's Fighting Ships*, p.24.
8 'Barbados Defence Force', *Aeroflight*, <http://www.aeroflight.co.uk/ops/mil/barbados-defence-force.htm>.
9 Ivelaw Lloyd Griffith, *The Quest for Security in the Caribbean*, p.120.
10 '2 Guilty in New Orleans for plot on Dominica invasion', *The New York Times* (21 June 1981).
11 Mark Adkin, *Urgent Fury: The Battle for Grenada* (London: Leo Cooper, 1989), p.92.
12 Mark Adkin, *Urgent Fury*, pp.92–93.
13 Mark Adkin, *Urgent Fury*, pp.92–93.
14 Mark Adkin, *Urgent Fury*, pp.92–99.
15 Mark Adkin, *Urgent Fury*, pp.92–99.
16 Mark Adkin, *Urgent Fury*, p.93.
17 Mark Adkin, *Urgent Fury*, p.94.
18 Mark Adkin, *Urgent Fury*, pp.94–95.
19 Mark Adkin, *Urgent Fury*, pp.119–130.
20 Mark Adkin, *Urgent Fury*, pp.129–130.
21 Mark Adkin, *Urgent Fury*, p.219.
22 'The Caribbean Defence and Security', <http://www.resdal.org/ing/assets/atlas_2016_ing_08.pdf>.
23 Reserves include two rifle companies and a coast guard reserve – rifle companies do not exceed seventy personnel.
24 Rifles are now largely M16 variants but the British variant of the FN MAG GPMG is widely employed at section and platoon level.
25 Ivelaw Lloyd Griffith, *The Quest for Security in the Caribbean*, pp.118–123.
26 <https://www.barbadosparliament.com/.../44a64e31bf71ca9b9a02346b2b1fa3a6.pdf>, and Resolution Supplementary Estimates, No. 6, 2013–2014.
27 <https://www.barbadostoday.bb/2016/01/16/big-haul/>.
28 <https://www.barbadosparliament.com/.../44a64e31bf71ca9b9a02346b2b1fa3a6.pdf>.
29 'IAI ELTA Awarded Contract to Upgrade Barbados Coastal Surveillance Systems & Facilities', *Armada International* (7 May 2019), <https://armadainternational.com/2019/05/iai-elta-awarded-contract-to-upgrade-barbados-coastal-surveillance-systems-facilities/>.

Chapter 4

1 Overall total population, 'World Population Prospects: The 2019 Revision'
2 Guyana Census Compendium 2012, <https://statisticsguyana.gov.gy/wp-content/uploads/2019/11/Final_2012_Census_Compendium2.pdf>.
3 'Political and Economic History of Guyana', *SJSU*, <https://www.sjsu.edu/faculty/watkins/guyana.htm>.
4 'Political and Economic History of Guyana', *SJSU*, <https://www.sjsu.edu/faculty/watkins/guyana.htm>.
5 Janine Mendes-Franco, 'Appeal court says the answer to Guyana's election results lies in the recount', *Global Voices* (31 July 2020),

<https://globalvoices.org/2020/07/31/appeal-court-says-the-answer-to-guyanas-election-results-lies-in-the-recount/>.
6 D. Zwaagstra, 'Essequibo, the Territorial Dispute between Venezuela and Guyana', *Peace Palace Library* (8 January 2016), <https://www.peacepalacelibrary.nl/2016/01/essequibo-the-territorial-dispute-between-venezuela-and-guyana/>.
7 D. Zwaagstra, 'Essequibo, the Territorial Dispute between Venezuela and Guyana'.
8 'Gov't protests after Venezuela holds oil research boat', *Stabroek News* (12 October 2013), <https://www.stabroeknews.com/2013/10/12/news/guyana/govt-protests-after-venezuela-holds-oil-research-boat/>.
9 'Guyana says Exxon to begin offshore drilling, Venezuela irked', *Reuters*, accessed 8 Jun. 2015.
10 'Canciller guyanés convocará a embajadora venezolana', *El Universal* (8 June 2015).
11 'Venezuela navy confronts Exxon oil ship in Guyana border dispute', *Reuters* (23 December 2018).
12 'Guyana says two Venezuelan fighter jets flew over its airspace', *Reuters* (3 March 2021).
13 Guyana v Suriname, Award, ICGJ 370 (PCA 2007), 17 September 2007, Permanent Court of Arbitration [PCA]
14 'Guyana Army History', *Global Security.org*.
15 'Guyana Army History', *Global Security.org*.
16 'Guyana Army History', *Global Security.org*.
17 Compton Hartley Liverpool, *Foundation of the Guyana Defence Force: A Soldier of Valour Story* (AuthorHouse 2016; Kindle edition), p.40.
18 Compton Hartley Liverpool, *Foundation of the Guyana Defence Force*, p.102.
19 'History of the 21 Artillery Company', defunct Guyana Defence Force website (author's notes).
20 'History of the 21 Artillery Company'.
21 'History of the 21 Artillery Company'.
22 'History of the 21 Artillery Company'.
23 'History of the 21 Artillery Company'.
24 'Guyana Defence Force', *Aeroflight*, <http://www.aeroflight.co.uk/ops/mil/guyana-defence-force.htm>.
25 'Guyana Defence Force', *Aeroflight*.
26 'All-Time Aircraft Used List Guyana Defence Force', *Aeroflight*, <http://www.aeroflight.co.uk/user/every/guyana-df-all-time-aircraft-list.htm>.
27 Compton Hartley Liverpool, *Foundation of the Guyana Defence Force*, pp.181–184.
28 Compton Hartley Liverpool, *Foundation of the Guyana Defence Force*, pp.182–184.
29 Compton Hartley Liverpool, *Foundation of the Guyana Defence Force*, pp.182–184.
30 Compton Hartley Liverpool, *Foundation of the Guyana Defence Force*, pp.182–184.
31 Compton Hartley Liverpool, *Foundation of the Guyana Defence Force*, pp.182–184.
32 Compton Hartley Liverpool, *Foundation of the Guyana Defence Force*, pp.182–184.
33 Compton Hartley Liverpool, *Foundation of the Guyana Defence Force*, pp.182–184.
34 Compton Hartley Liverpool, *Foundation of the Guyana Defence Force*, pp.182–184.
35 'Amerindian News', *Georgetown*, 2:3 (15 May 1968).
36 Manuel Felipe Sierra, 'Guyana: from Rupununi to the Hague', *Eneltapete* (7 April 2020), <https://www.eneltapete.com/historia/1407/guyana-de-rupununi-a-la-haya>.
37 D. Granger, 'The Rupununi Rebellion, 1969', *Stabroek News* (18 January 2009), <https://www.stabroeknews.com/2009/01/18/features/the-rupununi-rebellion-1969/>.
38 D. Granger, 'The Defence of the New River, 1967-1969', *Stabroek News* (15 February 2009), <https://www.stabroeknews.com/2009/02/15/features/the-defence-of-the-new-river-1967-1969/>.
39 D. Granger, 'The Defence of the New River, 1967-1969'.
40 D. Granger, 'The Defence of the New River, 1967-1969'.
41 P. Jardim, 'Guyana Defends Itself', *Guyana Then and Now*, <https://guyanathenandnow.wordpress.com/british-guiana-airways-limited/>.
42 P. Jardim, 'Guyana Defends Itself'.
43 Michael Chan-A-Sue, 'The Guns of August', *Guyana Loop*, <https://guyana.hoop.la/topic/the-guns-of-august>.
44 D. Granger, 'The Defence of the New River, 1967-1969'.
45 G.K. Danns, *Domination and Power in Guyana* (New Brunswick: Transaction Books, 1982), pp.117–118.
46 G.K. Danns, *Domination and Power*, pp.119–120.
47 *Report of the British Guiana Commission of Inquiry*, p.49.
48 PPP newspaper, *The Mirror* (10 June 1973).
49 G.K. Danns, *Domination and Power*, pp.120–122.
50 G.K. Danns, *Domination and Power*, pp.58–66.
51 C. Singh, *Guyana: Politics in a Plantation Society* (Stanford: Praeger Publ. 1988), pp.76–77.
52 C. Singh, *Guyana: Politics in a Plantation Society*, pp.70–85.
53 G.K. Danns, *Domination and Power*, pp.122–125.
54 G.K. Danns, *Domination and Power*, pp.122–125.
55 G.K. Danns, *Domination and Power*, pp.122–125.
56 'A policeman died in 1973', *Kaiteur News* (1 April 2015), <https://www.kaieteurnewsonline.com/2015/04/01/a-policeman-died-in-1973/>.
57 C. Singh, *Guyana: Politics in a Plantation Society*, pp.76–105.
58 Unofficial pdf copy of the Disciplined Forces Commission Report, May 2004 (obtained by the author), p.196.
59 Unofficial pdf copy of the Disciplined Forces Commission Report, p.89.
60 'GDF pledges "loyalty" to "democratically elected" government, Commander-in-Chief', *Demerara Waves* (3 August 2020), <https://demerarawaves.com/2020/08/03/gdf-pledges-loyalty-to-democratically-elected-government-commander-in-chief/>.
61 'Guyana Defence Force', *Global Security.org*.
62 '1,608 persons recruited to Guyana People's Militia – Min. Harmon', *Department of Public Information* (19 July 2018).
63 'Guyana Army', *Global Security.org*.
64 'Guyana Army', *Global Security.org*.
65 'GDF Skyvans arrive', *Guyana Chronicle* (29 June 2019), <https://guyanachronicle.com/2019/06/29/gdf-skyvans-arrive>.
66 'Guyana Defence Force Skyvans arrive', *Demerara Waves* (28 June 2019), <https://demerarawaves.com/2019/06/28/guyana-defence-force-skyvans-arrive/>.
67 G. Reim, 'Bell approved to sell two 412EPI and two 429 helicopters to Guyana', *Flight Global* (30 October 2020), <https://www.flightglobal.com/helicopters/bell-approved-to-sell-two-412epi-and-two-429-helicopters-to-guyana/140906.article>.
68 Julieta Pelcastre, 'Guyana Receives Bell 412 Helicopter to Improve Air Security', *Dialogo Americas* (26 April 2021), <https://dialogo-americas.com/articles/guyana-receives-bell-412-helicopter-to-improve-air-security/>.
69 'Acquisition of Bell 412EPI helicopter boosts Guyana's security – Army Chief", *iNews Guyana* (14 March 2021), <https://www.inewsguyana.com/acquisition-of-bell-412epi-helicopter-boosts-guyanas-security-army-chief/>.
70 'GDF Coast Guard to get more vessels this year', *Demerara Waves* (13 March 2021), <https://demerarawaves.com/2021/03/13/gdf-coast-guard-to-get-more-vessels-this-year/>.

Chapter 5

1 *Jamaica Population 2021, World Population Review* <https://worldpopulationreview.com/countries/jamaica-population>.
2 'Mission', *Jamaica Defence Force*, <https://www.jdfweb.com/mission/>.
3 'More Police Welcome', *The Jamaica Gleaner* (9 September 2019), <https://jamaica-gleaner.com/article/commentary/20190909/editorial-more-police-welcome>.
4 'History', *Jamaica Defence Force*, <https://www.jdfweb.com/history/>.
5 'History', *Jamaica Defence Force*.

6 'History', *Jamaica Defence Force.*
7 The West Indies Federation, *CARICOM*, <https://caricom.org/the-west-indies-federation/>.
8 Humphrey Metzgen and John Graham, *Caribbean Wars Untold: A Salute to the British West Indies* (2007), ISBN 9766402035, ISBN 9789766402037.
9 Terry Lacey, *Violence and politics in Jamaica 1960-1970: internal security in developing country*, 1977, ISBN 0719006333, ISBN 9780719006333, p.107.
10 Terry Lacey, *Violence and politics in Jamaica 1960-1970*, p.107
11 Terry Lacey, *Violence and politics in Jamaica 1960-1970*, pp.105–115.
12 'History', *Jamaica Defence Force.*
13 'Jamaica Regiment', *Global Security.org*, <https://www.globalsecurity.org/military/world/caribbean/jm-regiment.htm>.
14 'Jamaica Regiment', *Global Security.*
15 'Jamaica Regiment', *Global Security.*
16 'Jamaica Regiment', *Global Security.*
17 'Jamaica Regiment', *Global Security.*
18 'Jamaica Regiment', *Global Security.*
19 'JDF to Acquire New Fleet of Armoured Vehicles', *Jamaica Information Service* (3 December 2013), <https://jis.gov.jm/jdf-acquire-new-fleet-armoured-vehicles/>.
20 'Jamaica Defence Force', *Aeroflight*, <http://www.aeroflight.co.uk/ops/mil/jamaican-defence-force.htm>.
21 'Jamaica Defence Force', *Aeroflight.*
22 'Jamaica Defence Force', *Aeroflight.*
23 'Jamaica Defence Force', *Aeroflight.*
24 'All-Time Aircraft Used List Jamaican Defence Force', *Aeroflight*, <http://www.aeroflight.co.uk/user/every/jamaica-df-all-time-aircraft-used-listing.htm>.
25 '1st District Jamaica Defence Force Coast Guard', *Jamaica Defence Force*, <https://www.jdfweb.com/1st-dist-jdf-coast-guard/>.
26 '1st District Jamaica Defence Force Coast Guard', *Jamaica Defence Force.*
27 *Conway's All the World's Fighting Ships*, p.219.
28 Ivelaw Lloyd Griffith, *The Quest for Security in the Caribbean*, p.136.
29 Joint History Office of the Chairman of the Joint Chiefs of Staff, *Operation Urgent Fury* (CreateSpace Independent Publishing Platform 2014), p.36.
30 Edgar F. Raines, *The Rucksack War* (Washington: Center for Military History, 2010), p.356.
31 *West Kingston Commission of Inquiry* (Government of Jamaica, 2014), pp.36–39.
32 *West Kingston Commission of Inquiry*, pp.41–42.
33 *West Kingston Commission of Inquiry*, pp.42–43.
34 *West Kingston Commission of Inquiry*, p.44.
35 *West Kingston Commission of Inquiry*, pp.45–48.
36 *West Kingston Commission of Inquiry*, pp.60–62.
37 *West Kingston Commission of Inquiry*, p.61.
38 *West Kingston Commission of Inquiry*, p.65.
39 *West Kingston Commission of Inquiry*, p.73.
40 *West Kingston Commission of Inquiry*, p.74.
41 *West Kingston Commission of Inquiry*, pp.76–77.
42 *West Kingston Commission of Inquiry*, p.78.
43 *West Kingston Commission of Inquiry*, p.80.
44 *West Kingston Commission of Inquiry*, pp.156–157.
45 *West Kingston Commission of Inquiry*, p.330, and pp.334–335.
46 *West Kingston Commission of Inquiry*, p.433.
47 *West Kingston Commission of Inquiry*, p.15.
48 'Organization', *Jamaica Defence Force*, <https://www.jdfweb.com/organization/>.
49 Jamaica Defence Force – Jamaica Regiment', *Jamaica Defence Force*, <https://www.jdfweb.com/jamaica-regiment/>.
50 Jamaica Defence Force – Jamaica Regiment', *Jamaica Defence Force*, <https://www.jdfweb.com/jamaica-regiment/>.
51 'National Reserves called out amid crime wave', *Jamaica* Star (23 September 2016), <http://jamaica-star.com/article/20160923/national-reserves-called-out-amid-crime-wave>.
52 'Jamaica Regiment', *Jamaica Defence Force*, <https://www.jdfweb.com/1st-bn-the-jamaica-regiment/>.
53 Sanjay Badri-Maharaj, 'The Jamaica Defence Force – Balancing Priorities with Resources', *IDSA*, <https://idsa.in/idsacomments/the-jamaica-defence-force_sbmaharaj_091216>.
54 'Combat Support Battalion', *Jamaica Defence Force*, <https://www.jdfweb.com/combat-support-bn/>.
55 'Support Brigade', *Jamaica Defence Force*, <https://www.jdfweb.com/support-brigade/>.
56 '1 Engineer Regiment (JDF)', *Jamaica Defence Force*, <https://www.jdfweb.com/1-engineer-regiment-jdf/>.
57 'National Reserve', *Jamaica Defence Force*, <https://www.jdfweb.com/jamaica-national-reserve/>.
58 'Maritime, Air and Cyber Command', *Jamaica Defence Force*, <https://www.jdfweb.com/maritime-air-and-cyber-command/>.
59 John Duke & Lloyd Horrigan, *Vertical Mag* (10 September 2020), <https://verticalmag.com/features/pilots-of-the-caribbean-the-jamaica-defense-force-airs-out-its-bell-429s/>.
60 John Duke & Lloyd Horrigan, *Vertical Mag.*
61 John Duke & Lloyd Horrigan, *Vertical Mag.*
62 John Duke & Lloyd Horrigan, *Vertical Mag.*
63 'Bell announces sale of six Bell 505s to Jamaica Defence Force', *Vertical Mag* (8 February 2021), <https://verticalmag.com/press-releases/bell-announces-sale-bell-505-jamaica-defence-force/>.
64 'JDF Acquires New Surveillance Aircraft', *Jamaica Information Service* (16 November 2018), <https://jis.gov.jm/jdf-acquires-new-surveillance-aircraft/>.
65 'Jamaica acquires four offshore patrol vehicles, two maritime aircraft', *Stabroek News* (26 June 2020), <https://www.stabroeknews.com/2020/06/26/news/regional/jamaica/jamaica-acquires-four-offshore-patrol-vehicles-two-maritime-aircraft/>.
66 'Decommissioning ceremony for Her Majesty Jamaica Ship Paul Bogle (P8)', *Jamaica Defence Force*, <https://www.jdfweb.com/the-official-handing-over-and-renaming-ceremony/>.
67 'Jamaica Defence Force Coast Guard (JDF CG)', *Global Security*, <https://www.globalsecurity.org/military/world/caribbean/jm-coast-guard.htm>.
68 'JDF now boasts Caribbean's largest maritime presence', *Jamaica Gleaner* (29 October 2017), <https://jamaica-gleaner.com/article/auto/20171029/jdf-now-boasts-caribbeans-largest-maritime-presence>.
69 'Facilitating collaborative commonality in the Caribbean with patrol boats', *Damen Magazine* (January 2021), <https://www.damen.com/en/magazines/2021/01/increasing-caribbean-capabilities-offshore-patrol-vessels>.
70 'Facilitating collaborative commonality in the Caribbean with patrol boats'.
71 'Facilitating collaborative commonality in the Caribbean with patrol boats'.
72 Mateo Natalucci, 'Jamaica orders Thales's coastal surveillance system', *Janes.com*, <https://www.janes.com/defence-news/news-detail/jamaica-orders-thaless-coastal-surveillance-system>.

Chapter 6

1 Trinidad and Tobago Literacy, <http://www.indexmundi.com/trinidad_and_tobago/literacy.html>.
2 'IMF World Economic Outlook Data', *International Monetary Fund*, <http://www.imf.org/external/pubs/ft/weo/2015/01/weodata/weorept.aspx?sy=2014&ey=2019&scsm=1&ssd=1&sort=country&ds=.&br= 1&pr1.x=73&pr1.y=10&c=369&s=NGDPD 2CNGDPDPC 2CPPPGDP 2CPPPPC&grp=0&a>.
3 'Trinidad and Tobago Demographic Report 2011', *Central Statistical Office*, <http://cso.planning.gov.tt/sites/default/files/content/images/census/TRINIDAD%20AND%20TOBAGO%202011%20Demographic%20Report.pdfhttp://www.trinidadexpress.com/news/Census__Mixed_population_on_the_rise-191944721.html>, p.15.
4 'Trinidad and Tobago Demographic Report 2011', *Central Statistical Office*, pp.17–18.

5 Ivelaw Lloyd Griffith, *Drugs and Security in the Caribbean: Sovereignty Under Siege* (Pennsylvania: Penn State Press, 1997), pp.47–48.
6 Ivelaw Lloyd Griffith, *Drugs and Security in the Caribbean*, p.69.
7 Ivelaw Lloyd Griffith, *Drugs and Security in the Caribbean*, p.84.
8 Ivelaw Lloyd Griffith, *Drugs and Security in the Caribbean*, pp.119–120.
9 '89 Trinis join Isis fighters', *Trinidad Guardian* (16 November 2016), <http://www.guardian.co.tt/news/2015-11-16/89-trinis-join-isis-fighters>.
10 G. Alexander, 'Serious threat to T&T', *Trinidad Guardian* (15 April 2016), <http://www.guardian.co.tt/news/2016-04-15/serious-threat-tt>.
11 G. Alexander, 'Govt to meet Muslims on Isis', *Trinidad Guardian* (7 August 2016), <http://www.guardian.co.tt/news/2016-08-07/govt-meet-muslims-isis>.
12 C. Kissoon, 'Trini children in ISIS recruitment video', *Trinidad Express* (6 November 2016) <http://www.trinidadexpress.com/20151106/news/trini-children-in-isis-recruitment-video>.
13 Ivelaw Lloyd Griffith, *The Quest for Security in the Caribbean*, p.109.
14 Stewart Hylton Edwards, *Lengthening Shadows: Birth and Revolt of the Trinidad Army* (Port of Spain: Inprint Caribbean, 1982), p.22.
15 Stewart Hylton Edwards, *Lengthening Shadows*, p.33.
16 Stewart Hylton Edwards, *Lengthening Shadows*, p.30.
17 Stewart Hylton Edwards, *Lengthening Shadows*, p.31.
18 Stewart Hylton Edwards, *Lengthening Shadows*, p.100.
19 Raffique Shah, 'Takeover of Teteron ...one shot was all it took', <http://www.trinicenter.com/1970/Blackpower5.htm>.
20 Raffique Shah, 'Takeover of Teteron ...one shot was all it took'.
21 Raffique Shah, 'Takeover of Teteron ...one shot was all it took'.
22 Raffique Shah, 'Takeover of Teteron ...one shot was all it took'.
23 Raffique Shah, 'Panic in the city', <http://www.trinicenter.com/1970/Blackpower6.htm>.
24 Raffique Shah, 'The People Have Absolved Me', in S. Ryan (ed.), *Power: The Black Power Revolution 1970* (St Augustine: ISER, 1995), p.482.
25 Raffique Shah, 'Panic in the city'.
26 Raffique Shah, 'Battle for the hillside', <http://www.trinicenter.com/1970/Blackpower7.htm>.
27 Raffique Shah, 'Battle for the hillside'.
28 Raffique Shah, 'Battle for the hillside'.
29 Raffique Shah, 'Battle for the hillside'.
30 Raffique Shah, 'Weapons down, amnesty for all', <http://www.trinicenter.com/1970/Blackpower8.htm>.
31 For a fuller account of the events described here, see Sanjay Badri-Maharaj, *Trinidad 1990: The Caribbean's Islamist Insurrection* (Warwick: Helion & Company, 2020)
32 Author's research – visual identification of both weapons and equipment.
33 Author's research – visual identification of both weapons and equipment.
34 Sanjay Badri-Maharaj, 'Rebuilding the Trinidad and Tobago Coast Guard', *Institute for Defence Studies and Analyses* (26 August 2016), <https://idsa.in/idsacomments/rebuilding-the-trinidad-and-tobago-coast-guard_sbmaharaj_260816>.
35 Sanjay Badri-Maharaj, 'Rebuilding the Trinidad and Tobago Coast Guard', *Institute for Defence Studies and Analyses* (26 August 2016), <https://idsa.in/idsacomments/rebuilding-the-trinidad-and-tobago-coast-guard_sbmaharaj_260816>.
36 Sanjay Badri-Maharaj, 'Rebuilding the Trinidad and Tobago Coast Guard'.
37 D.J. O'Dowd, *Review of the Trinidad and Tobago Police Service* (Unpublished, May 1991), Chapter 11, para 3.5, subpara 3.1.1.
38 Sanjay Badri-Maharaj, 'Trinidad and Tobago – An Emerging Security Scenario', *Air Combat Information Group* (29 December 2011), <https://web.archive.org/web/20120723075914/http://www.acig.info/CMS/index.php?option=com_content&task=view&id=258&Itemid=47>.
39 Trinidad and Tobago Parliament, *Report of the Commission of Enquiry into the 1990 attempted coup*, <http://ttparliament.org/documents/rptcoe1990.pdf>.
40 Trinidad and Tobago Parliament, *Report of the Commission of Enquiry into the 1990 attempted coup*.
41 Trinidad and Tobago Parliament, *Report of the Commission of Enquiry into the 1990 attempted coup*, pp.258–259.
42 Trinidad and Tobago Parliament, *Report of the Commission of Enquiry into the 1990 attempted coup*, pp.56–57.
43 E.T.V. Furlonge-Kelly, *The Silent Victory* (Port of Spain: Golden Eagle, 1991), p.33.
44 Trinidad and Tobago Parliament, *Report of the Commission of Enquiry into the 1990 attempted coup*, pp.251–254.
45 Trinidad and Tobago Parliament, *Report of the Commission of Enquiry into the 1990 attempted coup*, pp.251–254.
46 Trinidad and Tobago Parliament, *Report of the Commission of Enquiry into the 1990 attempted coup*, pp.385–390.
47 Trinidad and Tobago Parliament, *Report of the Commission of Enquiry into the 1990 attempted coup*, pp.385–386.
48 Trinidad and Tobago Parliament, *Report of the Commission of Enquiry into the 1990 attempted coup*, p.335.
49 Trinidad and Tobago Parliament, *Report of the Commission of Enquiry into the 1990 attempted coup*, pp.265–266.
50 Trinidad and Tobago Parliament, *Report of the Commission of Enquiry into the 1990 attempted coup*, pp.274–282.
51 Trinidad and Tobago Parliament, *Report of the Commission of Enquiry into the 1990 attempted coup*, p.246.
52 Trinidad and Tobago Parliament, *Report of the Commission of Enquiry into the 1990 attempted coup*, p.148.
53 Interview with Major General Ralph Brown (22 September 1999).
54 *Report to the Minister of Justice and National Security*, prepared by Joseph Theodore (23 August 1990).
55 S. Ryan, *The Muslimeen Grab for Power* (Port of Spain: Inprint, 1991), p.158.
56 Trinidad and Tobago Parliament, *Report of the Commission of Enquiry into the 1990 attempted coup*, p.150.
57 Trinidad and Tobago Parliament, *Report of the Commission of Enquiry into the 1990 attempted coup*, pp.877–878.
58 Trinidad and Tobago Parliament, *Report of the Commission of Enquiry into the 1990 attempted coup*, p.888.
59 Trinidad and Tobago Parliament, *Report of the Commission of Enquiry into the 1990 attempted coup*, p.889.
60 Trinidad and Tobago Parliament, *Report of the Commission of Enquiry into the 1990 attempted coup*, p.889.
61 Trinidad and Tobago Parliament, *Report of the Commission of Enquiry into the 1990 attempted coup*, pp.880–895.
62 Trinidad and Tobago Parliament, *Report of the Commission of Enquiry into the 1990 attempted coup*, pp.888–891.
63 Trinidad and Tobago Parliament, *Report of the Commission of Enquiry into the 1990 attempted coup*, pp.888–891.
64 Trinidad and Tobago Parliament, *Report of the Commission of Enquiry into the 1990 attempted coup*, pp.888–891.
65 Trinidad and Tobago Parliament, *Report of the Commission of Enquiry into the 1990 attempted coup*, pp.154–157.
66 Trinidad and Tobago Parliament, *Report of the Commission of Enquiry into the 1990 attempted coup*, pp.154–157.
67 Trinidad and Tobago Parliament, *Report of the Commission of Enquiry into the 1990 attempted coup*, pp.154–157.
68 Trinidad and Tobago Parliament, *Report of the Commission of Enquiry into the 1990 attempted coup*, pp.154–157.
69 Trinidad and Tobago Parliament, *Report of the Commission of Enquiry into the 1990 attempted coup*, pp.154–157.
70 Trinidad and Tobago Parliament, *Report of the Commission of Enquiry into the 1990 attempted coup*, pp.154–157.
71 Trinidad and Tobago Parliament, *Report of the Commission of Enquiry into the 1990 attempted coup*, p.7.
72 Sanjay Badri-Maharaj, 'Rebuilding the Trinidad and Tobago Coast Guard', *IDSA* (26 August 2016), <http://idsa.in/idsacomments/rebuilding-the-trinidad-and-tobago-coast-guard_sbmaharaj_260816>.

73 Sanjay Badri-Maharaj, 'Trinidad and Tobago Coast Guard and the Australian Connection', *IDSA* (8 June 2018), <https://www.idsa.in/idsacomments/trinidad-and-tobago-coast-guard-and-australian_sbmaharaj-080619>.

74 Sanjay Badri-Maharaj 'How the SPa was Chosen – The Trinidad and Tobago Coast Guard's DAMEN SPa 5009 fleet', *Chuck Hill's CG Blog* (18 March 2018), <https://chuckhillscgblog.net/2018/03/18/how-the-spa-was-chosen-the-trinidad-and-tobago-coast-guards-damen-spa-5009-fleet/>.

75 Sanjay Badri-Maharaj 'How the SPa was Chosen – The Trinidad and Tobago Coast Guard's DAMEN SPa 5009 fleet', *Chuck Hill's CG Blog* (18 March 2018), <https://chuckhillscgblog.net/2018/03/18/how-the-spa-was-chosen-the-trinidad-and-tobago-coast-guards-damen-spa-5009-fleet/>.

76 Sanjay Badri-Maharaj 'How the SPa was Chosen – The Trinidad and Tobago Coast Guard's DAMEN SPa 5009 fleet', *Chuck Hill's CG Blog* (18 March 2018), <https://chuckhillscgblog.net/2018/03/18/how-the-spa-was-chosen-the-trinidad-and-tobago-coast-guards-damen-spa-5009-fleet/>.

77 Sanjay Badri-Maharaj, 'Trinidad and Tobago's Maritime Security: Myths and Reality', *The Kootneeti* (29 July 2020), <https://thekootneeti.in/2020/07/29/trinidad-and-tobagos-maritime-security-myths-and-reality/>.

78 Sanjay Badri-Maharaj, 'Trinidad and Tobago's Maritime Security: Myths and Reality', *The Kootneeti* (29 July 2020), <https://thekootneeti.in/2020/07/29/trinidad-and-tobagos-maritime-security-myths-and-reality/>.

79 'Austal Australia launches first of two cape-class patrol boats for Trinidad and Tobago coast guard', *Austal* (4 December 2020), <https://www.austal.com/news/austal-australia-launches-first-two-cape-class-patrol-boats-trinidad-and-tobago-coast-guard>.

80 Sanjay Badri-Maharaj, 'Trinidad and Tobago's Air Arms: Inefficient Duplication of Effort', *IDSA* (21 September 2016), <http://idsa.in/idsacomments/trinidad-and-tobagos-air-arms_sbmaharaj_210916>.

81 Sanjay Badri-Maharaj, 'Trinidad and Tobago – An Emerging Security Scenario'.

82 Sanjay Badri-Maharaj, 'Trinidad and Tobago – An Emerging Security Scenario'.

83 Sanjay Badri-Maharaj, 'Trinidad and Tobago's Air Arms: Inefficient Duplication of Effort'.

84 Sanjay Badri-Maharaj, 'Trinidad and Tobago's Air Arms: Inefficient Duplication of Effort'.

85 Darlisha Ghouralal, 'Helicopters grounded: $200m maintenance too costly', *Loop TT* (30 June 2017), <http://www.looptt.com/content/helicopters-grounded-200m-maintenance-too-costly>.

86 'Trinidad and Tobago Air Guard Helicopters grounded as government refuses $28.75 million maintenance obligation', *Helicopter News Wire* (13 July 2017), <http://helicopternewswire.com/trinidad-tobago-air-guard-helicopters-grounded-government-refuses-28-75-million-maintenance-obligation>, accessed 5 April 2018.

87 Telephone conversation with NOC Air Division Senior Pilot, 24 November 2017.

88 Anna Ramdass, 'Govt faces legal action over contract for helicopters, hangar', *Trinidad Express* (13 October 2017), <https://www.trinidadexpress.com/news/local/govt-faces-legal-action-over-contract-for-helicopters-hangar/article_305c4f1f-25af-54d9-9b13-997ba36b881c.html>.

89 Khamal Georges, 'Pay protest at Air Division grounds security copters', *Trinidad Guardian* (27 February 2018), <http://www.guardian.co.tt/news/2018-02-26/pay-protest-air-division-grounds-security-copters>.

ABOUT THE AUTHOR

Sanjay Badri-Maharaj, from Trinidad and Tobago, received his MA and PhD from the epartment of War Studies, Kings College London. His thesis was on India's Nuclear Weapons Program. He has written and published extensively, including *The Armageddon Factor: Nuclear Weapons in the India-Pakistan Context* (2000) and *Indian Nuclear Strategy: Confronting the Potential Nuclear Threat from both Pakistan and China* (2018), as well as *Kargil 1999, Trinidad 1990, Operation Meghdoot* and *Nuclear India* for Helion's @War series. He has served as a consultant to the Ministry of National Security in Trinidad and was a visiting International Fellow at the Institute for Defence Studies and Analyses, New Delhi.